Week 7 — Summer Practice — P 119 - 136

Day 1	Groups Of Odd And Even Numbers	....	
	Use an apostrophe	....	
	Daily Challenge 🌐		
Day 2	Addition Using Rectangular Arrays	....	122
	Spelling patterns	....	123
	Daily Challenge 🌐		
Day 3	Three Digit Numbers	....	125
	Consult reference materials	....	126
	Daily Challenge 🌐		
Day 4	Count In Hundreds	....	128
	Use knowledge of language and its conventions	....	129
	Daily Challenge 🌐		
Day 5	Count Within 1000	....	131
	Formal and Informal language	....	132
	Daily Challenge 🌐		
Cross Word Puzzles		....	134

🌐 Online Activity	Reading Assignment	Vocabulary Practice	Summer Diary

Week 8 — Summer Practice — P 137 - 152

Day 1	Compare Two Three-digit Numbers	....	137
	Prefix and Suffix	....	138
	Daily Challenge 🌐		
Day 2	Add And Subtract Within 100 Using Place Values	....	140
	Adjectives and Adverbs	....	141
	Daily Challenge 🌐		
Day 3	Add Four Two-digit Numbers	....	143
	The context clue	....	144
	Daily Challenge 🌐		
Day 4	Add And Subtract Within 1000	....	146
	Roots and affixes	....	147
	Daily Challenge 🌐		
Day 5	Mental Addition And Subtraction In Steps Of 10	....	149
	Connecting related words	....	150
	Daily Challenge 🌐		

🌐 Online Activity	Reading Assignment	Vocabulary Practice	Summer Diary

Week 9

9

Summer Practice

P 153 - 169

	Bundle Of Tens	153
Day 1	The meaning of words	155
	Daily Challenge 🌐	
	Measuring Length Of Objects	157
Day 2	Usage of words	158
	Daily Challenge 🌐	
	Measure Length Of Object Using Two Different Length Units	160
Day 3	Shades of word meaning	161
	Daily Challenge 🌐	
	Estimate Lengths Using Different Units Of Measurement	162
Day 4	Vocabulary acquisition	163
	Daily Challenge 🌐	
	Compare The Length Of Objects	165
Day 5	Introducing and Closing Topics and connecting ideas	167
	Daily Challenge 🌐	

🌐 Online Activity | Reading Assignment | Vocabulary Practice | Summer Diary

Week 10 **Lumos Short Story Competition 2022**

Details of Lumos Short Story Competition 2022 170

Winning Stories from 2021 & 2020 172

Answer Key and Detailed Explanation **174**

Blogs

- Stop! In The Name Of Education: Prevent Summer Learning Loss With 7 Simple Steps 220
- Summer Reading: Questions To Ask That Promote Comprehension 222
- Beating The Brain Drain Through Literacy: Webinar Recap With Printable Activity Sheet 224
- Summer Is Here! Keep Your Child's Writing Skills Sharp With Online Games 227
- Webinar "cliff Notes" For Beating Summer Academic Loss: An Informative Guide To Parents 228
- Valuable Learning Experiences: A Summer Activity Guide For Parents 231

Additional Information **233**

Table of Contents

Introduction				1
		How to Use This Workbook Effectively During Summer		6

Summer Practice and Fun Activities

Week 1
Summer Practice
P 9 - 25

Day 1	Solve Addition And Subtraction Problems	9
	The Question Session	10
	Daily Challenge ⊕	
Day 2	Addition And Subtraction Problems	12
	Recount stories	13
	Daily Challenge ⊕	
Day 3	Groups Of Odd And Even Numbers	15
	Describing Characters	16
	Daily Challenge ⊕	
Day 4	Addition Using Rectangular Arrays	18
	Figurative Language	19
	Daily Challenge ⊕	
Day 5	Three Digit Numbers	21
	How is it Written?	22
	Daily Challenge ⊕	

Learn Sign Language	24

⊕ Online Activity | Reading Assignment | Vocabulary Practice | Summer Diary

Week 2
Summer Practice
P 26 - 48

Day 1	Count In Hundreds	26
	Point of View	31
	Daily Challenge ⊕	
Day 2	Count Within 1000	33
	I Can See It!	34
	Daily Challenge ⊕	
Day 3	Read And Write Numbers To 1000 Using Base-ten Numerals	36
	Alike and Different	37
	Daily Challenge ⊕	
Day 4	Compare Two Three-digit Numbers	40
	Ask and answer questions	41
	Daily Challenge ⊕	
Day 5	Add And Subtract Within 100 Using Place Values	43
	The Main idea	44
	Daily Challenge ⊕	

7 Simple Ways To Improve Your Road Skating	46

⊕ Online Activity | Reading Assignment | Vocabulary Practice | Summer Diary

Week 5 Summer Practice P 85 - 101

Day 1	Represent Whole Numbers As Lengths On A Number Line	85
	Use context to find the meaning of words	86
	Daily Challenge 🌐	
Day 2	Tell And Write Time From Clocks	88
	People, Places, and Things	89
	Daily Challenge 🌐	
Day 3	Solve Word Problems Involving Money	91
	Language conventions	92
	Daily Challenge 🌐	
Day 4	Generate Measurement Data	94
	Regular and Irregular Plural Nouns	95
	Daily Challenge 🌐	
Day 5	Draw Graphs To Represent Data	97
	Reflexive pronouns	98
	Daily Challenge 🌐	
Maze Game		100

🌐 Online Activity | Reading Assignment | Vocabulary Practice | Summer Diary

Week 6 Summer Practice P 102 - 118

Day 1	Recognize And Draw Shapes	102
	Past tense of verbs	103
	Daily Challenge 🌐	
Day 2	Partition a Rectangle Into Rows And Columns	105
	Simple and compound sentences	106
	Daily Challenge 🌐	
Day 3	Partition Circles And Rectangles	109
	Understand Language conventions	110
	Daily Challenge 🌐	
Day 4	Solve Addition And Subtraction Problems	112
	How is it Capitalized?	113
	Daily Challenge 🌐	
Day 5	Addition And Subtraction Problems	115
	The Comma and Quotation Dilemma	116
	Daily Challenge 🌐	

🌐 Online Activity | Reading Assignment | Vocabulary Practice | Summer Diary

Week 3 — Summer Practice — P 49 - 65

Day 1
- Add Four Two-digit Numbers 49
- Connect the dots 50
- Daily Challenge 🌐

Day 2
- Add And Subtract Within 1000 52
- What Does It Mean? 52
- Daily Challenge 🌐

Day 3
- Mental Addition And Subtraction In Steps Of 10 54
- Special Text Parts 55
- Daily Challenge 🌐

Day 4
- Explain Why - Addition And Subtraction Strategies Work 57
- The main purpose of a text 58
- Daily Challenge 🌐

Day 5
- Bundle Of Tens 60
- Informational illustration 61
- Daily Challenge 🌐

Draw and Color 63

🌐 Online Activity | Reading Assignment | Vocabulary Practice | Summer Diary

Week 4 — Summer Practice — P 66 - 84

Day 1
- Measuring Length Of Objects 66
- Reason it out 68
- Daily Challenge 🌐

Day 2
- Measure Length Of Object Using Two Different Length Units 70
- Compare and contrast 71
- Daily Challenge 🌐

Day 3
- Estimate Lengths Using Different Units Of Measurement 73
- Decode the words 74
- Daily Challenge 🌐

Day 4
- Compare The Length Of Objects 76
- Comprehend the text 77
- Daily Challenge 🌐

Day 5
- Addition And Subtraction Word Problems Within 100 79
- Understand the purpose of the text 80
- Daily Challenge 🌐

Swimming: 7 Tips to Become a Better Swimmer 82

🌐 Online Activity | Reading Assignment | Vocabulary Practice | Summer Diary

Lumos Summer Learning HeadStart, Grade 2 to 3: Fun Activities, Math, Reading, Vocabulary, Writing and Language Practice

Contributing Author   - Bonnie McRae
Contributing Author   - Amber Williams
Contributing Author   - Mary Waters Cox
Executive Producer   - Mukunda Krishnaswamy
Database Administrator - R. Raghavendra Rao

First Edition - 2020

ISBN 13: 9781096631262

Printed in the United States of America

Last updated - April 2022

For permissions and additional information contact us

Lumos Information Services, LLC   Email: support@lumoslearning.com
PO Box 1575, Piscataway, NJ 08855-1575   Tel: (732) 384-0146
http://www.LumosLearning.com   Fax: (866) 283-6471

Developed by Expert Teachers

What is Summer Academic Learning Loss?

What is Summer Academic Learning Loss? Studies show that if students take a standardized test at the end of the school year, and then repeat that test when they return in the fall, they will lose approximately four to six weeks of learning. In other words, they could potentially miss more questions in the fall than they would in the spring. This loss is commonly referred to as the summer slide.

When these standardized testing scores drop an average of one month, it causes teachers to spend at least the first four to five weeks, on average, re-teaching critical material. In terms of math, students typically lose an average of two and a half months of skills, and when reading and math losses are combined, it averages three months; it may even be lower for students in lower-income homes.

And on average, the three areas students will typically lose ground in are spelling, vocabulary, and mathematics.

How can You Help Combat Summer Learning Loss?

Like anything, academics are something that requires practice, and if they are not used regularly, you run the risk of losing them. Because of this, it is imperative your children work to keep their minds sharp over the summer. There are many ways to keep your children engaged over the summer, and we're going to explore some of the most beneficial.

Start with School:

Your best source of information is your child's school. Have a conversation with your child's teacher. Tell them you are interested in working on some academics over the summer and ask what suggestions they might have. Be sure to ask about any areas your child may be struggling in and for a list of books to read over the summer. Also, talk to your child's counselor. They may have recommendations of local summer activities that will relate back to the schools and what your child needs to know. Finally, ask the front office staff for any information on currently existing after school programs (the counselor may also be able to provide this). Although after school programs may end shortly, the organizations running them will often have information on summer camps. Many of these are often free or at a very low cost to you and your family.

Stay Local:

Scour your local area for free or low-cost activities and events. Most museums will have dollar days of some kind where you can get money-off admission for going on a certain day of the week or a certain time. Zoos will often do the same thing. Take lunch to the park and eat outside, talking about the leaves, flowers, or anything else you can find there. Your child can pick one favorite thing and research it. Attend concerts or shows put on by local artists, musicians, or other vendors. There are many other options available; you just have to explore and find them. The key here is to engage your children. Have them look online with you or search the local newspapers/magazines. Allow them to plan the itinerary, or work with you on it, and when they get back, have them write a journal about the activity. Or, even better, have them write a letter or email to a family member about what they did.

Practice Daily:

Whether the choice is a family activity or experiencing the local environment, staying academically focused is the key is to keep your child engaged every day. This daily practice helps keep student's minds sharp and focused, ensuring they will be able to not only retain the knowledge they have learned, but in many cases begin to move ahead for the next year.

Summer Strategies for Students

Summer is here, which brings a time of excitement, relaxation, and fun. School is the last thing on your mind, but that doesn't mean learning has to be on vacation too. In fact, learning is as just as important and be just as fun (if not more) during the summer months than during the school year.

Did you know that during the summer:

- Students often lose an average of 2 and ½ months of math skills
- Students often lose 2 months of reading skills
- Teachers spend at least the first 4 to 5 weeks of the next school year reteaching important skills and concepts

Your brain is like a muscle, and like any muscle, it must be worked out regularly, and like this, your language arts and math skills are something that requires practice; if you do not use them regularly, you run the risk of losing them. So, it is very important you keep working through the summer. But, it doesn't always have to be 'school' type of work. There are many ways to stay engaged, and we're going to spend a little time looking through them.

Read and Write as Often as Possible

Reading is one of the most important things you can do to keep your brain sharp and engaged. Here are some tips to remember about summer reading:

- Often, summer is the perfect time to find and read new books or books you have always been curious about. However, without your teacher, you may struggle with finding a book that is appropriate for your reading level. In this case, you just have to remember the five-finger rule: open a book to a random page and begin reading aloud, holding up one finger for each word you cannot say or do not know. If you have more than five fingers visible, then the book is probably too hard to read.

- Reading goes beyond books; there are so many other ways to read. Magazines are a great way to keep kids connected to learning, and they encourage so many different activities. National Geographic Kids, Ranger Rick, and American Girl are just a few examples. As silly as it may sound, you can also read the backs of cereal boxes and billboards to work on reading confidence and fluency, and learn many new things along the way! And thinking completely outside the box, you can also read when singing karaoke. Reading the words as they flash across the screen is a great way to build fluency. You can also turn the closed captioning on when a TV show is on to encourage literacy and reading fluency.

But writing is equally as important, and there are many things you can do to write over the summer:

- First, consider keeping a journal of your summer activities. You can detail the things you do, places you go, even people you meet. Be sure to include as much description as possible – sights, sounds, colors should all be included so you can easily remember and visualize the images. But the wonderful thing about a journal is that spelling and sentence structure are not as important. It's just the practice of actually writing;   that is where your focus should be. The other nice thing about a journal is that this informal writing is just for you; with journal writing you don't have to worry about anything, you just have to start writing.

- But if you want a little more depth to your journaling, and you want to share it with others, there is a fantastic opportunity for you with blogging. With parental approval, you can create a blog online where you can share your summer experiences with friends, family, or any others. The wonderful thing about blogs is that you can play with the privacy settings and choose whom you want to see your blogs. You can make it private, where only the individuals who you send the link to can see it, or you can choose for it to be public where anyone can read it. Of course, if you are keeping a blog, you will have to make it a little more formal and pay attention to spelling, grammar, and sentences simply because you want to make sure your blog is pleasing to those who are reading it. Some popular places to post blogs are Blogger, Wordpress, Squarespace, and Quillpad.

Practice Math in Real Life

One way you can keep your brain sharp is by looking at the world around you and finding ways to include math. In this case, we're thinking of fun, practical ways to practice in your daily life.

- First, have some fun this summer with being in charge of some family projects. Suggest a fun project to complete with a parent or grandparent; decide on an area to plant some new bushes or maybe a small home project you can work on together. You can help design the project and maybe even research the best plants to plant or the best way to build the project. Then write the shopping list, making sure you determine the correct amount of supplies you will need. Without even realizing it, you would have used some basic math calculations and geometry to complete the project.

- You can also find math in shopping for groceries or while doing some back to school shopping. For each item that goes into the cart, estimate how much it will be and keep a running estimation of the total cost. Make it a competition before you go by estimating what your total bill will be and see who comes the closest. Or, you can even try and compete to see who can determine the correct total amount of tax that will be needed. And a final mental game to play while shopping is to determine the change you should receive when paying with cash. Not only is this a good skill to practice math, more importantly, helps you make sure you're getting the correct change.

- You can even use everyday math if you are doing any traveling this summer, and there are many fun ways to do this. Traveling requires money, and someone has to be in charge of the budget. You can volunteer to be the family accountant. Make a budget for the trip and keep all the receipts. Tally up the cost of the trip and even try to break it up by category – food, fun, hotels, gas are just a few of the categories you can include. For those of you who might be looking for even more of a challenge, you can calculate what percentage of your budget has been spent on each category as well.

- And traveling by car gives many opportunities as well. Use the car odometer to calculate how far you have traveled. For an added challenge, you can see if you can calculate how much gas you used as well as how many gallons of gas per mile have been used.

Practice Daily:

Whether the choice is a family activity or experiencing the local environment, staying academically focused is the key to keep your mind engaged every day. That daily practice keeps your brain sharp and focused, and helps to ensure that you are not only able to retain the knowledge you learned last year but also to get a jump start on next year's success too!

This book offers a variety of state standards aligned resources, in both printed and online format, to help students learn during Summer months.

The activities in the book are organized by week and aligned with the 2nd-grade learning standards. We encourage you to start at the beginning of Summer holidays. During each week, students can complete daily Math and English practice. There are five daily practice worksheets for each week. Students can log in to the online program once a week to complete reading, vocabulary and writing practice. Students can work on fun activity anytime during that week. Additionally, students can record their Summer activity through the online program.

Please note that the online program also includes access to third-grade learning resources. This section of the online program could be used to help students to get a glimpse of what they would be learning in the next grade level.

Weekly Fun Summer Photo Contest

Take a picture of your summer fun activity and share it on Twitter or Instagram

Use the **#SummerLearning** mention

@LumosLearning on Twitter or

@lumos.learning on Instagram

Tag friends and increase your chances of winning the contest

Participate and stand a chance to WIN $50 Amazon gift card!

Take Advantage of the Online Resources

To access the online resources included with this book, parents and teachers can register with a FREE account. With each free signup, student accounts can be associated to enable online access for them.

Once the registration is complete, the login credentials for the created accounts will be sent in email to the id used during signup. Students can log in to their student accounts to get started with their summer learning. Parents can use the parent portal to keep track of student's progress.

URL	QR Code
Visit the URL below for online registration **http://www.lumoslearning.com/a/tg2-3**	

Lumos Short Story Competition 2022

**Write a Short Story
Based On Your Summer Experiences**

Get A Chance To Win $100 Cash Prize
+
1 Year Free Subscription To Lumos StepUp
+
Trophy With Certificate

How can my child participate in this competition?

Step 1
Visit **www.lumoslearning.com/a/tg2-3** to register for online fun summer program.

Step 2
After registration, your child can upload their summer story by logging into the student portal and clicking on Lumos Short Story Competition 2022.
Last date for submission is August 31, 2022

How is this competition judged?
Lumos teachers will review students submissions in Sep 2022. Quality of submission would be judged based on creativity, coherence and writing skills.

We recommend short stories that are less than 500 words.

Solve Addition And Subtraction Problems (2.OA.A.1)

Day 1

1. Linda has 71 pages in her book. She read 23 pages. How many more pages does Linda have left to read?

   Ⓐ 52
   Ⓑ 94
   Ⓒ 58
   Ⓓ 48

2. Kim has 24 pieces of candy left after she gave 17 pieces to her classmate. How many pieces of candy did Kim have at first?

   Ⓐ 41
   Ⓑ 7
   Ⓒ 13
   Ⓓ 31

3. Lucy had 14 dollars and her father gave her 26. She went and bought an art kit for 15 dollars. How many dollars does Lucy have now?

   Ⓐ 40
   Ⓑ 25
   Ⓒ 9
   Ⓓ 55

4. Brad ate 11 grapes from a bag and Jay ate 14 grapes from the same bag. If there are 43 grapes remaining in the bag, how many grapes did the bag originally contain?

   Ⓐ 3
   Ⓑ 25
   Ⓒ 18
   Ⓓ 68

Day 1

One day, Sara's dad said they were going on a trip to the beach. Sara was happy! She got her things to go. First, she found her bathing suit. She put it on. Then, she went to the bathroom and picked out her best beach towel. Sara put it in her beach bag along with her sunscreen. Her mother told her to hurry up, dad was ready. She didn't want to forget her sand shovel and tools to make a sand castle. She quickly added them to her bag. Sara hurried when she heard her dad start the van.

It was a long drive to the beach. Dad played music on the radio. Mom sang along. Skip, their dog, even whined with the songs. Sara was smiling and having fun. At last, they were there. Dad said to help unload their van. Sara carefully took the picnic basket to the table that her Mom had found by the sand dunes.

It was so nice and warm at the beach. Skip ran to the water and jumped in. Dad, Mom and Sara laughed. Mom and Sara got in the water, too. The waves felt funny hitting Sara. She and Mom smiled. Dad was fishing close by. After a bit, Mom said they needed to stop to eat lunch. They ate hot dogs and chips. Skip ate one, too. Then, they rested.

Next, Sara and Dad made a sand castle. Skip laid down on it. That did not stop the fun. Dad said they could all go in one more time. Even Skip joined them. They jumped and swam in the ocean water for a long time. It was getting near dark. They had to leave to go home. Sara and Skip fell asleep on the way back. Everyone had a wonderful time at the beach!

5. Who went to the beach? Mark the correct answer.

Ⓐ Sara went to the beach with her parents.
Ⓑ Sara took her dog, Skip, on a trip to the beach.
Ⓒ Sara went to the beach with friends, Amy and Joan.
Ⓓ Sara, her parents and their dog, Skip, went to the beach.

6. Read the following sentence and question. Choose the best answer.
   Dad said they could all go in one more time.
   What was he talking about?

Ⓐ The table.
Ⓑ The van.
Ⓒ The water
Ⓓ None of the above.

7. Mark what Sara took to the beach in her bag. Mark all that are correct.

Ⓐ Dog leash
Ⓑ Sunscreen
Ⓒ Sand shovel and tools
Ⓓ Bathing suit
Ⓔ Shells
Ⓕ Purse
Ⓖ Beach Towel

8. Why do you think they decided to go home? Write your own sentence.

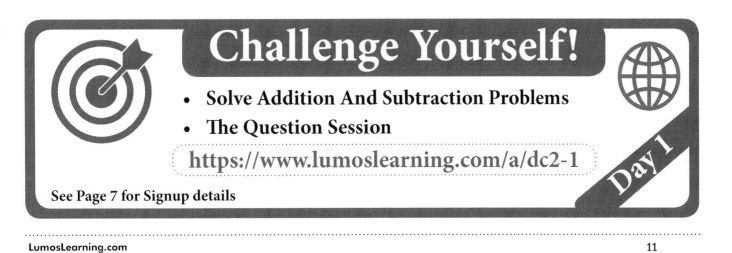

Day 2

1. Select TWO equations that equal the same sum.

    Ⓐ $12 + 4 = ?$
    Ⓑ $12 + 2 = ?$
    Ⓒ $3 + 13 = ?$
    Ⓓ $4 + 14 = ?$

2. Choose TWO equations that equal the same difference.

    Ⓐ $19 - 4 = ?$
    Ⓑ $15 - 8 = ?$
    Ⓒ $17 - 7 = ?$
    Ⓓ $20 - 13 = ?$

3. Select TWO equations that would equal the same number

    Ⓐ $12 - 8 = ?$
    Ⓑ $14 - 2 = ?$
    Ⓒ $9 + 3 = ?$
    Ⓓ $15 + 3 = ?$

4. Select all of the equations that have a sum of 20.

    Ⓐ $13 + 7 = ?$
    Ⓑ $8 + 12 = ?$
    Ⓒ $1 + 19 = ?$
    Ⓓ $4 + 6 = ?$
    Ⓔ $10 + 10 = ?$

The Rose Princess
An adaptation of the Rose Princess folk tale

Please read the story below and answer the questions that follow.

A long time ago in a faraway kingdom, there lived a beautiful princess. The princess had long red hair. She loved red roses. They called her Princess Rose.

At night-time, she would go out to her balcony. A golden bird would fly to her and sing. She would sing with the bird. The whole village would fall asleep and dream good thoughts.

There was an evil witch who did not like the princess. She cast a spell to turn the princess' hair black.

The next night when the golden bird came and sang, the princess sang again. This time, the village people went to sleep but had bad dreams.

The princess did not know what to do.

She asked the golden bird for help. The bird told her to dip her hair in rose water. The princess did, and it worked.

This made the witch even angrier. She cast a second spell.

This time she got rid of all the roses in the kingdom.

The princess asked the golden bird for help. The bird told her the same thing. The princess could not find any roses.

Just then a prince came with a lock of the princess' hair and dropped it on the ground. It grew into a rose bush full of roses. The princess had rose petals to put in the water and dipped her hair in. Her hair turned red again.

She could once again sing with the golden bird and make the people have good dreams.
The princess and prince got married. The evil witch was so upset, she left the kingdom.
They lived happily ever after.

5. **Write the sentences in the correct order to retell the story.**

Ⓐ The princess and prince got married and lived happily ever after.
Ⓑ The princess had long red hair and they called her the Rose Princess.
Ⓒ The bird told her how to get her red hair back again.
Ⓓ In the beginning, the princess and bird sang at night and the villagers had good dreams.

1	
2	
3	
4	

6. **What is the main meaning behind the folktale?**

Ⓐ There are all kinds of princesses.
Ⓑ Princesses always marry princes.
Ⓒ Birds are magical.
Ⓓ Good wins over evil.

7. **Mark the sentence that shows how the prince helped save the day for the princess and villagers.**

Ⓐ Just then a prince came with a lock of the princess' hair and dropped it on the ground.
Ⓑ Her hair turned red again.
Ⓒ They lived happily ever after.
Ⓓ The evil witch was upset.

8. **Which sentences do not go with the story? Mark all that apply.**

Ⓐ The bird sang with the princess at night.
Ⓑ The bird flew away to find the prince.
Ⓒ The witch was a good witch and loved the princess.
Ⓓ The prince saved the day

1. Which number below is an even number?

   Ⓐ 28
   Ⓑ 13
   Ⓒ 11
   Ⓓ 17

2. Select the equation that equals an even number

   Ⓐ 4+7=?
   Ⓑ 3+2=?
   Ⓒ 6+6=?
   Ⓓ 4+5=?

3. Select the equation that equals an odd number

   Ⓐ 3+3=?
   Ⓑ 10+10=?
   Ⓒ 4+8=?
   Ⓓ 3+6=?

4. James has an odd number of socks in his drawers. Choose the number below that could be the number of socks that James has.

   Ⓐ 22
   Ⓑ 48
   Ⓒ 17
   Ⓓ 30

Javier, Joseph, Wayne and Mike are good friends. They like playing baseball, fishing, hiking, and making model airplanes.

One day the boys wanted to try something new. They had seen the huge kites being flown over the lake. None of them had ever flown a kite.

Javier asked his dad what they needed to do to learn how to fly a kite. His dad told Javier they needed to start with learning how to fly small kites first.

They all got their money together and went to the hobby store. Javier and Wayne wanted kites that had dragons on them. Joseph and Mike liked the ones with long tails. The boys agreed on a dragon kite with a long tail.

Now to find the right spot to try it out. Another problem came up. Javier wanted to go to the lake and do it like they had seen the other kites being flown. Wayne said it was ok with him. It was ok with Joseph, too. Mike had a problem with the idea.
He wanted to do it in a park. He said the kite might go into the lake and fall in the water.

The boys talked about it. They made a list of things that could happen at the lake and things that could happen at the park.

The list showed them that the park was the best place. They went to the park. Their dragon kite went up high with its tail flying. They were so happy.

5. What did the boys decide they wanted to learn how to do?

- Ⓐ Go surfing
- Ⓑ Build a teepee
- Ⓒ Fly a kite
- Ⓓ Take swimming lessons

6. The boys had 2 problems in the story. What were they?

- Ⓐ Where to buy the kite
- Ⓑ What kind of kite to buy
- Ⓒ Where to fly the kite
- Ⓓ How much money to spend

7. How did the boys solve the first problem?

Ⓐ They decided to buy a cat kite.
Ⓑ They decided to buy a kite that had a dragon and had a long tail.
Ⓒ They decided they did not want to buy a kite.
Ⓓ They decided to buy a kite from a different store.

8. How did the boys solve the second problem? Mark the best answer from the story.

Ⓐ They made a list of things that could happen at the lake and things that could happen at the park. The list showed them that the park was the best place. They went to the park. Their dragon kite went up high with its tail flying.
Ⓑ Javier asked his dad what they needed to do to learn how to fly a kite. His dad told Javier they needed to start with learning how to fly small kites first.

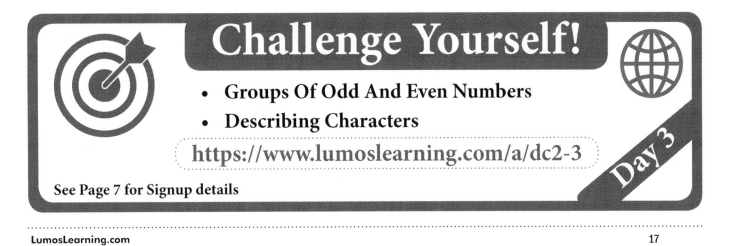

Challenge Yourself!

- **Groups Of Odd And Even Numbers**
- **Describing Characters**

https://www.lumoslearning.com/a/dc2-3

Day 3

See Page 7 for Signup details

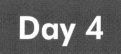 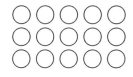

1. Choose the addition equation that represents the array.

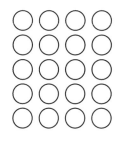

Ⓐ 3+3+3=?
Ⓑ 5+5+5+5+5=?
Ⓒ 5+5+5=?
Ⓓ 3+5=?

2. Choose the addition equation that represents the array.

Ⓐ 4+4+4+4+4=?
Ⓑ 5+5+5+5+5=?
Ⓒ 5+4=?
Ⓓ 4+4+5+5=?

3. Choose the addition equation that represents the array.

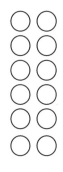

Ⓐ 2+2+6+6+6+6=?
Ⓑ 2+2+2+2+2+2=?
Ⓒ 6+2=?
Ⓓ 6+6+6+6+6+6=?

4. Select the array that equals 12.

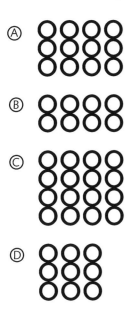

Ⓐ

Ⓑ

Ⓒ

Ⓓ

Figurative Language (RL.2.4)

Day 4

Going fishing

It's a great day to go fishing with Dad.
Get our poles and head to the lake.
Mom says -the bait -don't forget to take!
Spotty, the dog can't go-he's sad.

It's off to the lake, early in the day.
We stop near a shady, cool spot.
That way we won't get too hot.
Poles in the water to wait and hurray!

A bite first off, my pole dipping down.
Pulling and tucking, a keeper for sure!
Oh, no, don't take my lure!
What a big fish to take back to town!
A speckled fish, yellow and brown!

5. How do the rhymes help you better understand the poem? Choose the best answer

Ⓐ The rhyming words help by giving meaning to the poem and drawing pictures in your mind to understand it.
Ⓑ The rhyming words are not helpful.
Ⓒ The rhyming words make you think of things other than fishing.
Ⓓ The poem does not have rhyming words in it.

6. **What is the rhyming pattern for the first, second and third verses?**

  Ⓐ The first, third lines rhyme and the second and fourth lines.
  Ⓑ All lines rhyme in the poem.
  Ⓒ None of the lines rhyme.
  Ⓓ The first, fourth lines rhyme and the second,third lines rhyme.

7. **Which words in the poem rhyme with clown? Write them.**

8. **How can you make the following sentence more vivid? (Alliteration) Choose the best answer.**

  "A bite first off, my pole dipping down."

  Ⓐ A bite, my pole went down.
  Ⓑ A bite first off, my pole barely dipping down.
  Ⓒ A bite first off, my pole dipping dark deep down.
  Ⓓ None of the above.

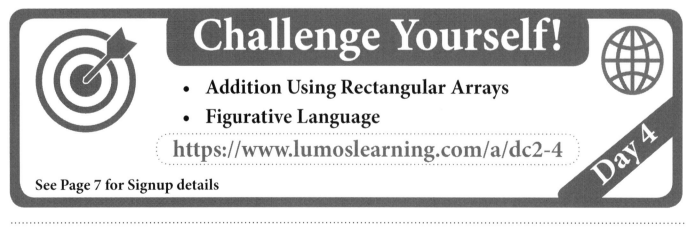

Challenge Yourself!

- **Addition Using Rectangular Arrays**
- **Figurative Language**

https://www.lumoslearning.com/a/dc2-4

See Page 7 for Signup details

Day 4

Day 5

1. Which number has 4 hundreds, 3 ones, and 2 tens?

   - Ⓐ 432
   - Ⓑ 234
   - Ⓒ 423
   - Ⓓ 342

2. Jake wrote a number with 7 ones, 3 hundreds, and 2 tens. What number did Jake write?

   - Ⓐ 327
   - Ⓑ 372
   - Ⓒ 732
   - Ⓓ 237

3. Select the number that has 6 tens, 8 ones, and 5 hundreds.

   - Ⓐ 685
   - Ⓑ 586
   - Ⓒ 856
   - Ⓓ 568

4. Choose a number that does not have any hundreds.

   - Ⓐ 300
   - Ⓑ 58
   - Ⓒ 700
   - Ⓓ 900

Chloe was staying at her Nana and Grandpa's house. She loved to help feed the animals. Nana and Grandpa had horses, and chickens.

Every day, Grandpa would ask her to help him with the animals outside. He would feed the horses first. Then he would feed the chickens.

Grandpa was a tall cowboy. He would whistle for the horses to come. The horses would run fast to the fence. Chloe helped him put the horse feed in the buckets and get the hose to fill up the water troughs. She really liked doing that.

When it was time to feed the chickens, Grandpa first looked for eggs in the chicken coop. Then he would make a sound like chickens and put out their feed.

This time, Chloe got to put out the feed. As she was doing that, she heard a "peep, peep, peep" sound. She was very excited. Chloe told her Grandpa, "Grandpa, do you hear that sound? Is it a baby chick?"

Grandpa listened. He laughed and said, "Yes, Chloe. Now where is it ? Let's look."

They looked all around the pen.

Just then, Chloe saw the little yellow chick in a corner of the pen. "Here, Grandpa, here it is!", she shouted.

Grandpa came and slowly picked up the chick. Chloe thought it was so cute.

Grandpa put it in a coop by one of the hens. Soon the hen snuggled the baby chick.

Chloe was so happy! What fun it was to visit and be a help to her Grandpa.

5. How does the start of the story help you to understand the ending? Choose the best answer.

(A) Chloe is at her Nana and Grandpa's house and helps feed the animals outside, where she finds a baby chick.
(B) Chloe feeds the animals outside.
(C) Chloe likes to help.
(D) The start of the story does not help you understand the ending.

6. Put the story sentences in the correct order.

Ⓐ She hears a baby chick when she is feeding the chickens.
Ⓑ Chloe helps Grandpa feed and water the horses.
Ⓒ Chloe is staying at her Nana and Grandpa's house.
Ⓓ Grandpa picks up the baby chick and puts it by a hen

7. Why is it important that the story begins with where Chloe is? Write your own sentence to answer this question.

8. Which of the following does NOT happen in the story?

Ⓐ Chloe and Grandpa feed the horses and chickens.
Ⓑ Chloe hears a baby chick.
Ⓒ Grandpa will not let Chloe help feed the chicks.
Ⓓ Grandpa puts the baby chick in a coop by a hen.

Learn Sign Language

What is American Sign Language?

American Sign Language (ASL) is a complete, complex language that employs signs made by moving the hands combined with facial expressions and postures of the body. It is the primary language of many North Americans who are deaf and is one of several communication options used by people who are deaf or hard-of-hearing.

Where did ASL originate?

The exact beginnings of ASL are not clear, but some suggest that it arose more than 200 years ago from the intermixing of local sign languages and French Sign Language (LSF, or Langue des Signes Française). Today's ASL includes some elements of LSF plus the original local sign languages, which over the years have melded and changed into a rich, complex, and mature language. Modern ASL and modern LSF are distinct languages and, while they still contain some similar signs, can no longer be understood by each other's users.

Source: https://www.nidcd.nih.gov/health/american-sign-language

Why should one learn sign language?

Enrich your cognitive skills: Sign language can enrich the cognitive development of a child. Since, different cognitive skills can be acquired as a child, learning sign language, can be implemented with practice and training in early childhood.

Make new friends: You could communicate better with the hearing-impaired people you meet, if you know the sign language, it is easier to understand and communicate effectively.

Volunteer: Use your ASL skills to interpret as a volunteer. volunteers can help in making a real difference in people's lives, with their time, effort and commitment.

Bilingual: If you are monolingual, here is an opportunity to become bilingual, with a cause.

Private chat: It would be useful to converse with a friend or in a group without anyone understanding, what you are up to.

Let's Learn the Alphabets

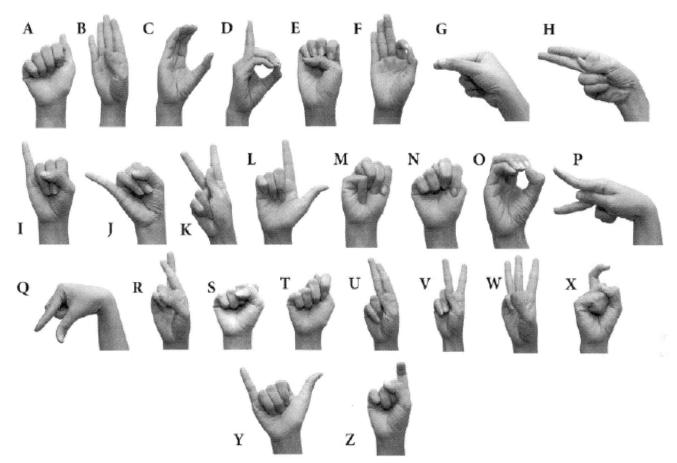

Sign language is fun if it is practiced with friends!
Partner with your friends or family members and try the following activities.

Activity

1. Communicate the following to your friend using the ASL.
   - USA
   - ASL

If your friend hasn't mastered the ASL yet, give the above alphabet chart to your friend.

2. Try saying your name in ASL using the hand gestures.

3. Have your friend communicate a funny word using ASL and you try to read it without the help of the chart. List the words you tried below.

Let's Learn the Numbers

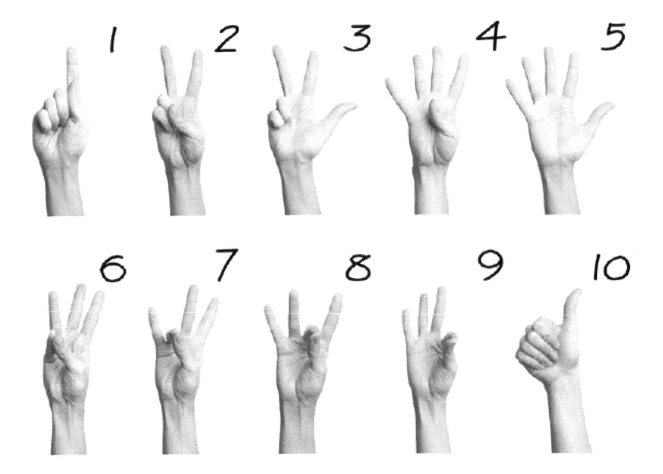

Activity:

1. Share your postal code through ASL to your friend.
2. Communicate your home phone number in ASL to your friend.

Let's Learn Some Words

RED

ORANGE

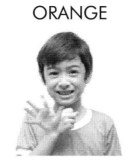

YELLOW

GREEN

PURPLE

BLUE

EAT

DRINK

MORE

PLEASE

THANK YOU

SORRY

This Week's Online Activities

- **Reading Assignment**
- **Vocabulary Practice**
- **Write Your Summer Diary**

https://www.lumoslearning.com/a/slh2-3

See Page 7 for Signup details

Weekly Fun Summer Photo Contest

Take a picture of your summer fun activity and share it on Twitter or Instagram

Use the **#SummerLearning** mention

@LumosLearning on Twitter or

@lumos.learning on Instagram

Tag friends and increase your chances of winning the contest

Participate and stand a chance to WIN $50 Amazon gift card!

Count In Hundreds (2.NBT.A.1.B)

Day 1

1. There are 5 hundreds below. How many tens are there?

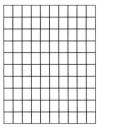

Ⓐ 50
Ⓑ 5
Ⓒ 500
Ⓓ 55

2. How many groups of 100 are below?

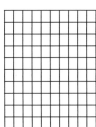

Ⓐ 30
Ⓑ 3
Ⓒ 300
Ⓓ 33

3. How many ones are shown below?

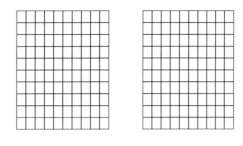

   Ⓐ 20
   Ⓑ 2
   Ⓒ 200
   Ⓓ 22

4. Which group shows 400?

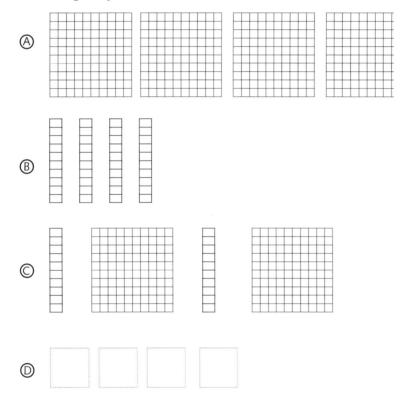

Day 1

Tabitha and Melony had just started ballet classes. The girls had their own ballet shoes and everything. Each Wednesday they went after school to Sally's School of Stars to practice.

"We love Ms. Sally!" Tabitha would say. "She's the best!"

"You got that right!" Melony would reply.

One day at practice, Tabitha took a fall.

"Yikes, my leg hurts!" She yelled.

"Oh, no!" replied Melony. "What happened?"

"Help me, please, get Ms. Sally, NOW!" cried Tabitha.

Melony ran to the front of the class and tugged at Ms. Sally.

"Dear, what is wrong?" asked Ms. Sally.

"HURRY! HURRY! HURRY! Tabitha is hurt BAD!" screamed Melony.

"OH, MY!"

Ms. Sally ran to find Tabitha.

Tabitha sat crying on the floor. "I don't know what happened." She whimpered. "It hurts really awful."

"Go get an ice pack for me, please, Melony. You know where they are, dear. Now, don't worry. I'm calling your mom on my cell, Tabitha." Ms. Sally said this in such a sweet calming voice. Tabitha quit crying when Melony put the ice pack where Ms. Sally said to put it. "Thanks," she said.

In a few minutes, Tabitha's mom came. She carried her to the car.

"Will you call us as soon as you know something, please?" asked Ms. Sally.

"Yes, of course," said Tabitha's mom.

Soon they got the call. It was just a sprained ankle. She would be fine in a few days.

"What a good thing to hear." sighed Ms. Sally.

5. How did Melony know that Tabitha was hurt? Which sentence helps you to know?

Ⓐ "We love Ms. Sally!"
Ⓑ "Thanks," she said.
Ⓒ "I don't know what happened."
Ⓓ "Help me, please, get Ms. Sally, NOW!" cried Tabitha.

6. What point of view (how the girls feel) is shown for Ms. Sally? Write your own sentence. Read the story again for help.

7. Pick two characteristics of Ms. Sally from the story narrative.

Ⓐ Ms. Sally was a kind and caring person.
Ⓑ Ms. Sally was not happy with the class.
Ⓒ Ms. Sally was worried about Tabitha getting hurt.
Ⓓ Ms. Sally did not listen to Melony.

8. Pretend that you are Melony. How would you say the following sentences?

"HURRY! HURRY! HURRY! Tabitha is hurt BAD!"

Ⓐ Very loud and with excitement
Ⓑ Very soft and calm
Ⓒ A little loud but not too much
Ⓓ Just read it, not loud or soft

Challenge Yourself!

- **Count In Hundreds**
- **Point of View**

https://www.lumoslearning.com/a/dc2-6

Day 1

See Page 7 for Signup details

Count Within 1000 (2.NBT.A.2)

1. **What number goes in the blank?**
   235, 240, 245, 250, ____

   (A) 5
   (B) 250
   (C) 260
   (D) 255

2. **What is the missing number?**
   200, ____, 400, 500

   (A) 300
   (B) 250
   (C) 600
   (D) 210

3. **Start at 67 and count up by tens. What is the 4th number?**
   67, ___, ____, ____, ____?

   (A) 77
   (B) 97
   (C) 467
   (D) 107

4. **Select all of the numbers you would say if you were counting by 5's from 0 to 100.**

   (A) 45
   (B) 54
   (C) 77
   (D) 80
   (E) 95

Mimi was Adelle's grandmother. Adelle liked going to her house in Georgia. Mimi had many things in her huge house. She had teapots, quilts, plates, and spoons.

Spoons were Adelle's favorite. Mimi had them in boxes and special ones hanging on the wall on a rack.

Mimi told stories of her spoons to Adelle. This was so much fun. Mimi loved spending time with her.

Mimi said, "Adelle, now look at these on the wall. They came from many places. Some are from states here in the U.S. Others are from far away countries I have visited."
Adelle replied, "Tell me, Mimi, tell me all about them."
She began, "Ok, let's see. There are ten spoons on this rack.

The first and last ones are from Finland. They were brought here by my grandmother. The second and sixth ones are from Denmark. We have family there, too. The third one is from Mississippi where I was born. The fourth one is from Texas where you live. The fifth one is just a fun one of Elvis. I loved his songs. The seventh one is from Arkansas, a very pretty place. The eighth one is from Pennsylvania. I went there with your mother once. The ninth one is from an Indian reservation in Oklahoma.

Mimi told me the stories of each of them. She had so many good stories to tell of the places she had been and family members.

5. Who are the characters in this story? List them.

6. Put the spoons in the right order as they appear in the picture (wall rack) and story.

1. Elvis
2. Denmark
3. Oklahoma
4. Arkansas
5. Mississippi
6. Finland
7. Texas
8. Pennsylvania
9. Finland
10. Denmark

7. What kind of relationship do Mimi and Adelle have? Write a sentence.

8. Which answer tells the setting of the story?

Ⓐ Mimi had them in boxes and special ones hanging on the wall on a rack.
Ⓑ Mimi told stories of her spoons to Adelle.
Ⓒ Adelle liked going to her house in Georgia. Mimi had many things in her huge house.
Ⓓ The first and last ones are from Finland.

Day 3

1. How is 458 written in expanded form?

   (A) 400 + 500 + 800
   (B) 45 + 8
   (C) 400 + 50 + 8
   (D) 400 + 58

2. Which number is five hundred thirty?

   (A) 503
   (B) 530
   (C) 533
   (D) 513

3. What is 200 + 8 written in standard form?

   (A) 280
   (B) 288
   (C) 208
   (D) 2008

4. What is 167 written in word form?

   (A) One hundred sixty-seven
   (B) One hundred six hundred seven
   (C) One hundred six seventy
   (D) One hundred sixty

Day 3

Story #1-Goldilocks and the Three Bears, adaptation version 1

Read the two stories and answer the questions. Reread as many times as you need to.

Once upon a time there were three bears, a papa, a mama and a baby. They were going to eat. Their porridge was too hot to eat, so they went for a walk.

Goldilocks came along and went into their house.

She was hungry and saw the food. Papa Bear's porridge was too hot. Mama Bear's porridge was too cold. Baby Bear's porridge was just right. She ate all of it!

Goldilocks wanted to rest. She saw 3 chairs. Papa Bear's chair was too hard. Mama Bear's chair was too soft. Baby Bear's chair was just right. But, Goldilocks broke it!

She was tired. Goldilocks saw 3 beds. Papa Bear's bed was too hard. Mama Bear's bed was too soft. Baby Bear's bed was just right. She went fast sleep.

Then, the 3 bears came home. They saw what happened to the porridge, the chair, and Goldilocks in the bed.

The bears roared.

Goldilocks woke up and jumped out of a window, running all the way home.

Story #2-Goldilocks, rewritten from memory

Once upon a time there were three bears who lived in a cottage in the woods. Papa Bear, Mama Bear and Baby Bear. The bears loved a good healthy breakfast. One morning, Mama Bear cooked porridge.

It was too hot to eat, so they went for a walk while it cooled off.

A pretty girl, Goldilocks, had gone into the woods alone. She smelled the food.

She went up to the cottage. No one answered her knock on the door. She went inside.

Here Goldilocks saw three bowls of porridge. She was hungry. She tried the first bowl. It was too hot.

She tried the second bowl. It was too cold. She tried the third bowl. It was just right. She ate it all!

Then she saw three chairs. She sat in the first chair. It was too hard. She tried the second chair. It was too soft. She sat in the third chair. It was just right, but it broke!

Goldilocks was getting very sleepy after eating all the porridge. She looked for a bed. She found three beds. The first bed was too high and the second was too low. The third bed was just right. She laid down and went to sleep.

The bears got home and saw their porridge. Papa Bear and Mama Bear said, "Someone's been eating my porridge". Baby Bear said, "Someone's been eating my porridge and it's all gone!"

Then they saw their chairs. Papa and Mama Bear said, "Someone's been sitting in my chair." Baby Bear said, "Someone's been sitting in my chair and it's broken!"

Now they decided to take naps. When they saw their beds, Papa Bear and Mama Bear said, "Someone's been sleeping in my bed." Baby Bear said, "Someone's been sleeping in my bed and she's still there

This woke Goldilocks! She was so scared. She ran out of the cottage and all the way home. She said she would never go far away alone again!

5. Why did the bears go for a walk?

Ⓐ They needed to check the forest.
Ⓑ They were doing their exercises.
Ⓒ Their porridge was too hot to eat.
Ⓓ They liked to go for walks.

6. Why did Goldilocks eat the porridge? Write your own sentence.

7. Where did the bears find Goldilocks?

Ⓐ Eating porridge
Ⓑ Walking around the cottage
Ⓒ Asleep in a bed
Ⓓ Sitting in a chair

8. Which sentence best tells about Goldilocks?

Ⓐ A pretty girl, Goldilocks, had gone into the woods alone.
Ⓑ She found three beds.
Ⓒ She sat in the first chair.
Ⓓ The third bed was just right.

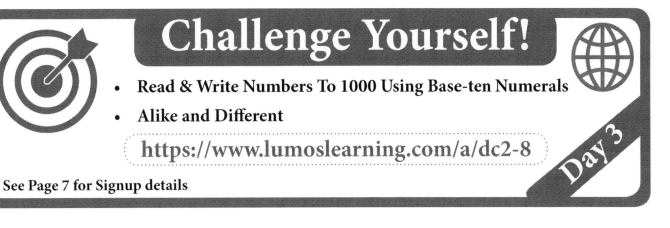

Challenge Yourself!

- Read & Write Numbers To 1000 Using Base-ten Numerals
- Alike and Different

https://www.lumoslearning.com/a/dc2-8

Day 3

See Page 7 for Signup details

Day 4

1. Choose the symbol that goes in the blank in the number sentence.

   458 _____ 485

   Ⓐ >
   Ⓑ <
   Ⓒ =

2. Choose the symbol that goes in the blank in the number sentence.

   276 _____ 267

   Ⓐ >
   Ⓑ <
   Ⓒ =

3. Choose the symbol that goes in the blank in the number sentence.

   408 _____ 480

   Ⓐ >
   Ⓑ <
   Ⓒ =

4. Choose the comparison that is correct.

   Ⓐ 212 > 221
   Ⓑ 986 < 968
   Ⓒ 521 = 512
   Ⓓ 761 > 716

This is a picture of a Barbeque (BBQ) pit. It is used for cooking many kinds of meat. Some kinds are beef, chicken, turkey, and pork.

They come in different sizes. This one is a large one. Some people use them for cooking during holidays, cook-off contests, big parties, and at restaurants. It can hold a huge amount of meat.

The pit is made of metal. It is a homemade pit. Homemade pits are made by people at their houses. They do not come from a store and are not made in a factory

It is placed on a trailer, so it can be moved around on wheels. This BBQ pit is too heavy to try to move without it being on a trailer.

It has an oven, a temperature gauge, a fire box and a smokestack. It also has a wood rack outside of the pit to place things on such as pans, and cooking utensils. The oven holds the meat on a rack. The temperature gauge shows how hot the oven is cooking. The fire box is where the wood is put and lit to make the heat in the oven. The smokestack is for the smoke to go out while it is cooking.

BBQ pits are very useful to many people.

5. What are some kinds of meat cooked on BBQ pits? Pick the best answer.

Ⓐ Chicken, turkey, and beef
Ⓑ Turkey and chicken
Ⓒ Beef, chicken, turkey and pork
Ⓓ Pork, and beef

6. How is a homemade BBQ pit different from one from a store?

Homemade pits are made by people at their ....They do not come from

a...............................and are not made in a ....

7. Why is a big BBQ pit placed on a trailer? Write your own sentence.

8. What is this passage about? Pick the best answer.

Ⓐ It tells about how to make a BBQ pit.
Ⓑ It tells the main information about a large BBQ pit.
Ⓒ It tells about how to cook on a BBQ pit.
Ⓓ It tells how to heat up a BBQ pit.

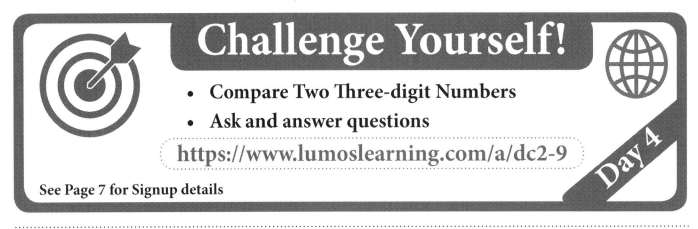

Challenge Yourself!

- **Compare Two Three-digit Numbers**
- **Ask and answer questions**

https://www.lumoslearning.com/a/dc2-9

See Page 7 for Signup details

Day 4

1. ? + 12 = 44

   Ⓐ 56
   Ⓑ 32
   Ⓒ 23
   Ⓓ 65

2. ? − 15 = 62

   Ⓐ 43
   Ⓑ 47
   Ⓒ 57
   Ⓓ 77

3. 21 + ? = 55

   Ⓐ 31
   Ⓑ 34
   Ⓒ 76
   Ⓓ 66

4. Select the equation that does NOT equal 76.

   Ⓐ 99 − 23 = ?
   Ⓑ 40 + 36 = ?
   Ⓒ 2 + 74 = ?
   Ⓓ 100 − 25 = ?

Day 5

Facts About Tropical Rainforests

Read the passage. Answer the questions. The paragraphs are numbered to help you with the questions.

1. Tropical rainforests are homes to many animals and people, and help support our lives. Rainforests are hot, rainy places with lots of huge trees. The plants have many leaves. They are found in places like Central and South America, Africa, Asia and Australia.

2. When scientists talk about rainforests, they talk about the three sections or layers of them. The bottom layer is called the "ground layer". Here live people, animals and plants. The ground is lush and damp. The next layer is the "understory" which is bushy. You can find trees and animals in this layer, too. The top is called the "canopy". It is very thick. Very little light gets in, so the rainforest is dark. The canopy is the protection for the rainforest.

3. If you look down from an airplane on a rainforest it looks like a big green carpet or green grass everywhere. The plants from the rainforests help the world to breathe. They make oxygen for us. We need this to breathe.

4. Many animals and insects live in rainforests on the bottom, understory or canopy levels. There are monkeys, parrots, toucans, birds, jaguars, snakes, butterflies, frogs, anteaters, and ants.

5. Beautiful plants live there, too. Flowers like hibiscus, orchid, and passion flower thrive in rainforests.

6. The rainforests are home to lakes, streams, and rivers. Here live other creatures like crocodiles, water lizards, turtles, snakes, and fish.

7. People in tribes have called the rainforests their home for centuries. They can find most everything they need to live on right in the rainforests.

8. Groups are helping to keep the rainforests alive for the people and animals there and for us to keep fresh air on earth.

5. What is the main topic of this article?

Ⓐ The article is about crocodiles.
Ⓑ The article is about tribes in rainforests.
Ⓒ The article is about how people are helping the rainforests.
Ⓓ The article gives facts about rainforests.

6. Fill in the blank to show the main topic.

_____ are homes to many animals, people, and help support our lives.

7. List the types of flowers in paragraph 5.

8. Fill in the chart with details from paragraph 4 and 6.

	Lives in water or on land	Land
snakes	☐	☐
monkeys	☐	☐
jaguars	☐	☐
parrots	☐	☐

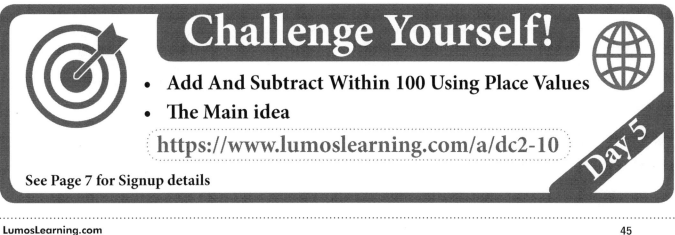

Challenge Yourself!

- **Add And Subtract Within 100 Using Place Values**
- **The Main idea**

  https://www.lumoslearning.com/a/dc2-10

Day 5

See Page 7 for Signup details

7 Simple Ways To Improve Your Road Skating

There is no better feeling than the freedom you feel from Road Skating. It is unlike anything else. The wind through your hair as you glide down the road on a beautiful sunny day. The breeze keeping you cool while you enjoy yourself. It is truly a magical feeling. Like anything else in life, you want to have fun while improving and be careful when you are playing. Here are seven simple ways to improve on your road skating.

1. Choosing the perfect skates for you

Before you can get out there and start skating, you need to decide what type of skates you want to wear. There are two different types of skates you can choose from. The first type of skates are called inline skates. These have four wheels together in a straight line, going down the middle, from the front to the back of the skate. They look similar to ice skates, but are for using outdoors or on a hard-wood surface. Inline skates are the more common of the two yet are a little harder to learn to use.

The second type of skates are called quad skates. Quads have two wheels in the front and two wheels in the back. Most quads will have a stopper in the front by the toe. This allows skaters to stop quicker and easier. Inline skates usually don't have a stopper, but there are some that do have one at the back of the skate.

Both skates have their strengths and weaknesses. Each type of skate has a unique feel to the way you skate in them. Some people don't like inlines because of the lack of feeling safe, others believe they are safer than skating with quads. You should try the two styles out and see what feels more natural for you.

2. Dress appropriately

It is important to dress appropriately. It seems like something you automatically do, but it is just as important as anything else. If it's a cool breezy day you might want to wear windbreaker pants and a t-shirt. On hot days, shorts would be a better dress option. Wearing a hat or sunglasses is useful in keeping the sun out of your eyes. Preparing an outfit for the day will help keep you cool outside.

3. Check the weather for the day

Weather will be a factor in deciding when to go out. It doesn't just factor in to how you dress. It also will determine if that day is good to skate at all. A beautiful day will bring hours of fun, but bad weather is never good. If there is in climate weather in the forecast then it may be a good idea to hold off on skating. Don't get caught in the rain because you forgot to check.

4. Safety first when skating

Safely skating is a good way to make sure that you can have a great time without any serious injuries. You should never go out without proper safety equipment. When getting ready, check and make sure you have everything you need. First thing you will need is a helmet. Helmets are a cool way to express yourself and keep your head safe. Helmets come in a variety of styles and colors, and can be a way to show your unique personality to everyone else around you.

Elbow pads and knee pads are also necessary when getting ready. When we are Road Skating we will fall from time to time. It happens to everyone and is just part of skating. Elbow pads and knee pads will help keep you unharmed whenever this happens. They keep us from getting scraped up, which doesn't feel so good. Wrist guards should be worn as well. Naturally, when we fall, we put our hands down to stop us. Wrist guards help protect your wrists from getting damaged when this happens.

5. Practice makes perfect: don't be scared to fail

Like anything in life, the more you practice something the easier it will come to you. It takes time and effort to become better at anything you do. We evolve everyday as we continue to strive to get better. Failure is something we have to deal with whenever working towards our goals. If everything in life comes easily then there would be no competitive spirit. The drive to be better makes things in life worth working towards. It is good to be scared sometimes. Fear brings out the best in you, but don't let it overwhelm you. If you fall, get back up and try again. In the moment it may seem pointless to continue, but the outcome will be rewarding.

6. Don't skate on an empty stomach and keep hydrated

Skating takes a lot of energy. Eating a good meal is very important when planning a day of roller exercise. Give yourself at least a half hour to digest your food before going out. Water is key too. Staying hydrated will keep you going throughout the day. It is important to have plenty of water ready as needed. Water and a good meal are essential.

7. Have fun while skating

Skating is meant to be fun. You should be able to be yourself and not worry about being judged by others. Just remember, if it wasn't fun then you probably wouldn't want to be doing it. Having fun while skating will make all that practice seem less like practice and more like an activity.

Following these simple guidelines will help you become a better skater. You will get better the more you practice, and having fun while doing it will make you want to practice more often. Everything will fall into place if you let it. Remember, we earn everything we get so how you go about getting there will determine the success you have in your attempts.

This Week's Online Activities

- Reading Assignment
- Vocabulary Practice
- Write Your Summer Diary

https://www.lumoslearning.com/a/slh2-3

See Page 7 for Signup details

Weekly Fun Summer Photo Contest

Take a picture of your summer fun activity and share it on Twitter or Instagram

Use the **#SummerLearning** mention

@LumosLearning on Twitter or

@lumos.learning on Instagram

Tag friends and increase your chances of winning the contest

Participate and stand a chance to WIN $50 Amazon gift card!

Week 3 Summer Practice

Add Four Two-digit Numbers (2.NBT.B.6)

1. Choose the correct sum for the equation
   $10 + 45 + 10 + 20 = ?$

   Ⓐ 75
   Ⓑ 85
   Ⓒ 55
   Ⓓ 80

2. Choose the correct sum for the equation
   $15 + 15 + 20 + 30 = ?$

   Ⓐ 80
   Ⓑ 30
   Ⓒ 50
   Ⓓ 75

3. Drew scored 12 points in the first game, 10 points in the second game, 16 points in the third game, and 8 points in the fourth game. How many total points did Drew score in all four games ?

   Ⓐ 26
   Ⓑ 12
   Ⓒ 22
   Ⓓ 46

4. What is the sum of 28, 31, 5, and 19?

   Ⓐ 84
   Ⓑ 48
   Ⓒ 83
   Ⓓ 78

Day 1

Read the story and answer the questions. Read it more than one time to better understand it.

George Washington was the first President of the United States. There are many events that led to this happening. He was born in Virginia on February 22,1732.

Our country was ruled by England.

George became a surveyor. This means that he did things like making maps.

He was also a farmer. His farm was called Mount Vernon.

George Washington married Martha Custis. She already had 2 children. He helped raise them.

People did not want to be a part of England. They wanted their own country. He joined these people. George was a general in the American Revolutionary Army.

He fought in the Revolutionary War to free America from England.
It was a long and hard fight. The colonists won the war.

The new country was named the United States of America.

George Washington was elected as the first President in 1789. He was a good man and very important person in the history of our country.

5. How did George Washington help our country? Pick 2 answers.

Ⓐ He became a surveyor
Ⓑ He fought in the American Revolutionary War
Ⓒ He got married.
Ⓓ He became the first President of the United States.

6. Who ruled America when George was born? Fill in the blank.

.... ruled America at that time.

7. Put the events in the right order to show how one led to another.

Ⓐ George Washington was important to our country.
Ⓑ George Washington joined the people in a war against England.
Ⓒ He was a general in the American Revolutionary War.
Ⓓ George Washington became President of the United States

```

```

8. Which of the sentences does NOT show how George Washington helped our country?

Ⓐ He lived on a farm named Mount Vernon.
Ⓑ He was important to our country.
Ⓒ He joined the fight against England.
Ⓓ He was President of the United States.

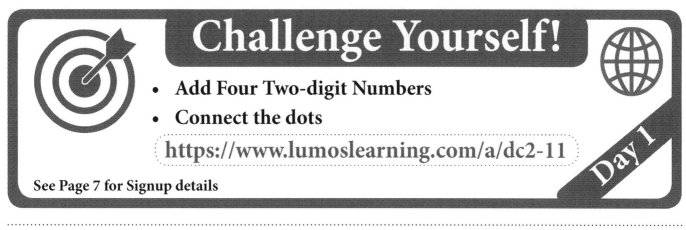

Challenge Yourself!

- **Add Four Two-digit Numbers**
- **Connect the dots**

https://www.lumoslearning.com/a/dc2-11

Day 1

See Page 7 for Signup details

Day 2

1. Solve: 763 – 211 = ?

    (A) 974
    (B) 551
    (C) 972
    (D) 552

2. Solve: 287 + 109 = ?

    (A) 396
    (B) 386
    (C) 392
    (D) 178

3. What is the sum of 418 and 220?

    (A) 198
    (B) 218
    (C) 638
    (D) 538

4. What is the difference between 733 and 190?

    (A) 543
    (B) 923
    (C) 663
    (D) 823

What Does It Mean? (RI.2.4)

Day 2

Read and answer the questions.

Have you ever heard the wind blowing? Have you looked up in the trees and seen the leaves moving? When air is moved around outside it is called wind. The wind can be stronger than the branches of a tree. Wind can <u>bend</u> the branches up and down and break trees. High winds can be dangerous to people and things. You can even hear wind howling as it moves from one area to another.

5. What is moving air called?

6. What does bend mean in the text?

① Ⓐ to run around
Ⓑ to move one way or another
Ⓒ to fix
Ⓓ to change color

Sound

Sound can travel. Sound must have **material** to go through like air, or water. When sound goes through air it is not as fast as if it goes through water. Sound moves 4 times quicker through water.

How fast? Scientists say that sound can go about 767miles an hour when it travels in water.

7. Which two words mean the same in the text? Pick two sets of words.

Ⓐ sound, material
Ⓑ fast, quicker
Ⓒ goes, moves
Ⓓ say, can

8. What examples of material are given in discussing sound?

Challenge Yourself!

- **Add And Subtract Within 1000**
- **What Does It Mean?**

https://www.lumoslearning.com/a/dc2-12

Day 2

See Page 7 for Signup details

Day 3

1. What number is 10 more than 458?

- Ⓐ 558
- Ⓑ 448
- Ⓒ 468
- Ⓓ 358

2. What is 100 less than 450?

- Ⓐ 350
- Ⓑ 550
- Ⓒ 340
- Ⓓ 540

3. 678 is 10 less than what number?

- Ⓐ 778
- Ⓑ 578
- Ⓒ 668
- Ⓓ 688

4. 743 is 100 more than what number?

- Ⓐ 753
- Ⓑ 843
- Ⓒ 643
- Ⓓ 733

Special Text Parts (RI.2.5)

Day 3

Read the glossary and the text. Answer the questions.

Citizen- a person living in a community.
Community - the area in which people live.
Congestion - blocked or slowed.
Rural - a farm or country community.
Store - a place where you buy things you need to live on or want.
Suburb - a community close by a city.
Transportation - ways to get from one place to another such as by bus, car, truck, subway, bicycle, train, or plane.
Urban - a city community where many businesses are located.

Citizens of communities do different things in their daily lives. The people in the urban community travel by many kinds of transportation. They often go from one area of the city to others. Some may take cars and then subways to work. Others hop on buses from their locations.

Those who live in the suburbs may find it more difficult to get into the city. Their time can be taken up by congestion on the freeways or searching for parking downtown. This might make them arrive late for work or meetings.

Rural citizens may not go into the city very often. They might raise their own goods. Farming and ranching are a part of their lives. There are some small stores in these areas. When rural citizens go to urban or suburban areas it will take them much longer to get there. They may have trouble finding their way around as urban communities may change. Most citizens of rural areas like living where there are no large businesses around them. They enjoy the peace and quietness of rural life.

Those living in urban and suburban communities have large stores or malls to go to when buying what they want or need. People living in different communities have different ways of living their daily lives.

5. Match the vocabulary words with their definitions.

	Country living	City living	Close to the city living
Urban	☐	☐	☐
Rural	☐	☐	☐
Suburban	☐	☐	☐

6. **Using the glossary to help you, why would congestion be a problem for those in the suburbs?**

   Ⓐ Congestion would be a problem because it might make them late for their jobs.
   Ⓑ Congestion would not be a problem because it would help them get to work faster
   Ⓒ Congestion would be a problem because they could not stop when they wanted to.
   Ⓓ Congestion would make it easier for them to listen to the radio.

7. **List the forms of transportation found in the glossary.**

8. **Tell what a citizen is?**

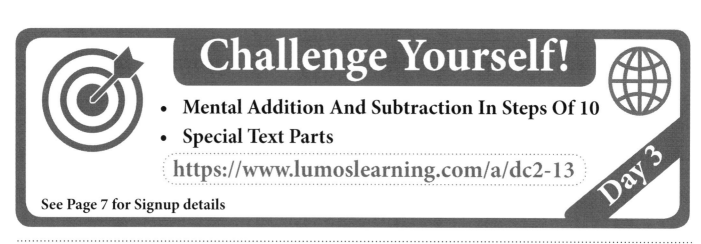

Challenge Yourself!

- **Mental Addition And Subtraction In Steps Of 10**
- **Special Text Parts**

https://www.lumoslearning.com/a/dc2-13

Day 3

See Page 7 for Signup details

Day 4

1. What is another way to add 43 + 16?

Ⓐ (40 + 10) + (3 + 6)
Ⓑ (40 + 1) + (30 + 6)
Ⓒ (34) + (61)
Ⓓ (4 + 1) + (30 + 60)

2. What is another way to add 27 + 12?

Ⓐ (20 + 70) + (1 + 2)
Ⓑ (20 + 10) + (7 + 2)
Ⓒ (71 + 22)
Ⓓ (72 + 21)

3. What is another way to add 31 + 67?

Ⓐ (60 + 30) + (1 + 7)
Ⓑ (6 + 3) + (70 + 40)
Ⓒ (30 + 6) + (40 + 7)
Ⓓ (43 + 76)

4. (40 + 10) + (6 + 5) could be another way to add which equation below?

Ⓐ 64 + 51 = ?
Ⓑ 14 + 9 = ?
Ⓒ 46 + 15 = ?
Ⓓ 406 + 105 = ?

The main purpose of a text (RI.8.1)

Owls are beautiful! Let's look at their characteristics.

Owls live in many places. Some live in rainforests, deserts, farms, marshes, woods, and on plains.

Owls can be seen in other places, too. The Snowy Owl and Hark Owl can stay in very cold weather.

They do not like the hot or wet weather.

Owls can make very loud noises. People know that owls can "hoot". Owls can make different sounds. They can shriek, hoot, bark, and even grunt like a pig. If they are upset, the noise can sound like clicking and hissing. Get away if you hear this sound when you are near an owl.

Most owls come out at night. They are nocturnal.

Owls have good eyes and even better hearing. They do not have a sense of smell.

Owls like to eat small prey. Owls fly then swoop down and pick their food up with their claws or beaks. They eat insects, snakes, mice, birds, squirrels, and rabbits depending on the kind of owl.

People have owls for pets, too. It is not easy to have a pet owl. You would need to read up on where to find owls to buy, what to keep them in, how to feed them and train them.

Owls are very interesting and beautiful birds.

5. What is the main idea of this passage?

Ⓐ Owls are nocturnal.
Ⓑ Owls have many characteristics.
Ⓒ Some people have owls as pets.
Ⓓ Owls have good hearing.

6. Fill in the chart to show the characteristics of owls. Mark yes or no.

	Yes	No
Nocturnal		
Can be pets		
Have good sense of smell		
Can make loud noises		

7. What is another word for "characteristic"? Read the words and definitions below and choose one.

Ⓐ Shrieking – loud noises, screaming, yelling
Ⓑ Trait - quality that makes something what it is, sets it apart from other things
Ⓒ Nocturnal- comes out at night, sleeps during the day
Ⓓ Swoops- dives down in a fast way

8. Think about the main idea. Pick 2 answers that are true about owls.

Ⓐ Owls usually come out in daylight.
Ⓑ Owls might sleep during the day.
Ⓒ Owls fly down to get their food.
Ⓓ Owls are not good at seeing or hearing.

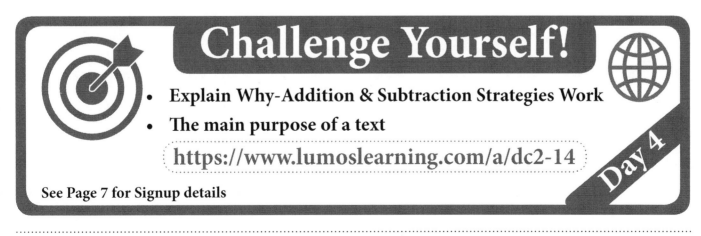

Challenge Yourself!

- Explain Why-Addition & Subtraction Strategies Work
- The main purpose of a text

https://www.lumoslearning.com/a/dc2-14

Day 4

See Page 7 for Signup details

Bundle Of Tens (2.NBT.A.1.A)

1. What number is represented below?

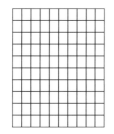 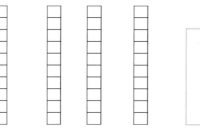

- Ⓐ 213
- Ⓑ 321
- Ⓒ 231
- Ⓓ 132

2. What number is 9 ones, 3 tens, 8 hundreds?

- Ⓐ 938
- Ⓑ 389
- Ⓒ 839
- Ⓓ 398

3. Which choice below is the same as 419?

- Ⓐ 1 hundred, 4 tens, 9 ones
- Ⓑ 9 ones, 4 hundreds, 1 ten
- Ⓒ 4 ones, 1 ten, 9 hundreds
- Ⓓ 1 hundred, 9 tens, 1 one

4. How many hundreds can be taken from 88 tens?

- Ⓐ 80
- Ⓑ 8
- Ⓒ 88
- Ⓓ 800

Day 5

Look at the pictures. Read the information. Answer the question.

A blind in a room

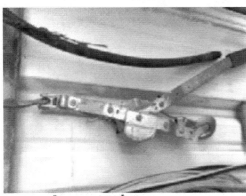

A come-along

A fishing pole

The Pulley- A simple machine

There are many kinds of simple machines. Simple machines make work easier. Pulleys are a kind of simple machine. They can be found in many things we use or see every day. Simple machines do not have a lot of parts. Pulleys are important in making work easier.

Look at the pictures. They all use pulleys. Pulleys come in many sizes. The size depends on the job to be done.

A pulley is a wheel. It is used with a rope, cord, belt or chain. If you pull on the rope, the other end goes up. Pulleys can make things go up and down and pull things. A flagpole runs on a pully. Construction cranes have pulleys. Have you ever seen someone raise a blind to see outside of a window? The blind runs on a pulley. The pictures show a blind in a room, a come-along, and a fishing pole. They all have pulleys.

Each type of pulley has a way to help make the job easier. The string on the blind is connected to the pulley and can raise or lower the blind. The come-along can be attached to a heavy object. By cranking the come-along, the pulley will move the object for you. With a fishing pole, the pulley helps to bring in the fishing line to make it easier to pull in the fish you catch.

Jobs and tasks would be much harder without the use of pulleys. Pulleys help people in many ways.

5. How do the pictures of objects using pulleys help you to understand the text?

Ⓐ The pictures along with the text do not help you at all.
Ⓑ The pictures along with the text show the pulley's working.
Ⓒ The pictures along with the text show you how to take apart pulleys.
Ⓓ The pictures along with the text give you a better understanding of how pulleys work in things.

6. What part of this text helps to clarify the meaning? Mark the best answer.

Ⓐ Pulleys are a kind of simple machine.
Ⓑ They can be found in many things we use or see every day.
Ⓒ Simple machines do not have a lot of parts.
Ⓓ Pulleys are important in making work easier.

7. Match the types of pulleys in the objects to their meaning.

	Helps to bring in your fish	Helps to raise or lower to see outside	Helps to move heavy objects
Blinds	☐	☐	☐
Come-along	☐	☐	☐
Fishing pole	☐	☐	☐

8. How do the pictures help you? Write your own sentence.

Challenge Yourself!

- **Bundle Of Tens**
- **Informational illustration**

https://www.lumoslearning.com/a/dc2-15

Day 5

See Page 7 for Signup details

Draw and Color

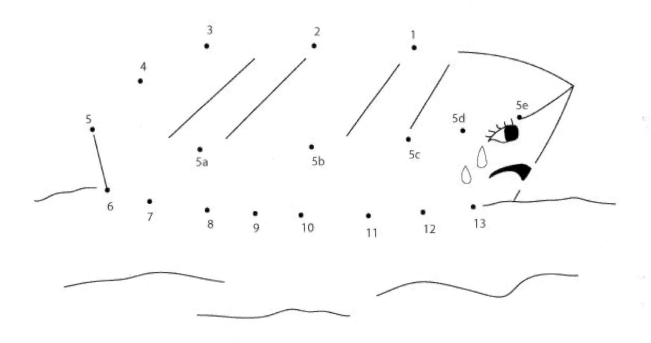

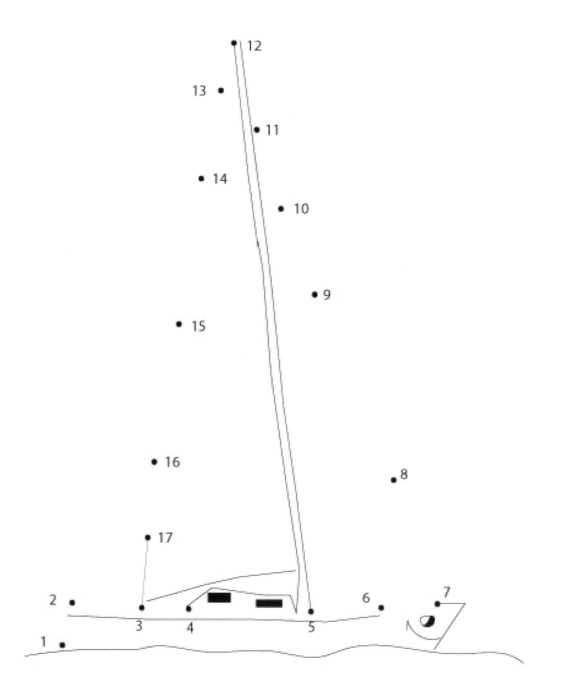

This Week's Online Activities

- **Reading Assignment**
- **Vocabulary Practice**
- **Write Your Summer Diary**

https://www.lumoslearning.com/a/slh2-3

See Page 7 for Signup details

Weekly Fun Summer Photo Contest

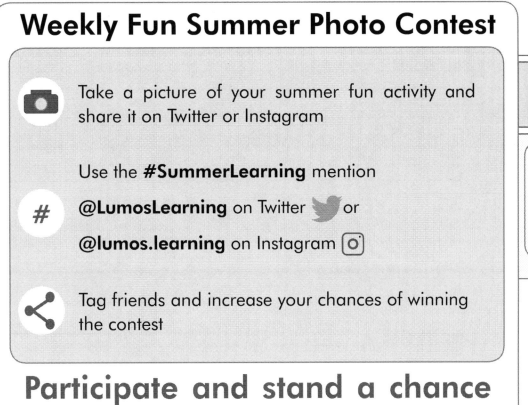

📷 Take a picture of your summer fun activity and share it on Twitter or Instagram

Use the **#SummerLearning** mention

**@LumosLearning** on Twitter 🐦 or

@lumos.learning on Instagram 📷

Tag friends and increase your chances of winning the contest

Participate and stand a chance to **WIN $50 Amazon gift card!**

Measuring Length Of Objects (2.MD.A.1)

1. How many inches long is the line below?

Ⓐ 8 inches
Ⓑ 18 inches
Ⓒ 80 inches
Ⓓ 1/8 inches

2. How many inches long is the line?

Ⓐ 9 inches
Ⓑ 2 inches
Ⓒ 7 inches
Ⓓ 12 inches

3. How many inches long is the line?

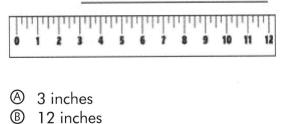

- Ⓐ 3 inches
- Ⓑ 12 inches
- Ⓒ 9 inches
- Ⓓ 36 inches

4. Brad cut a piece of string that is 4 inches. What choice below can represent Brad's string?

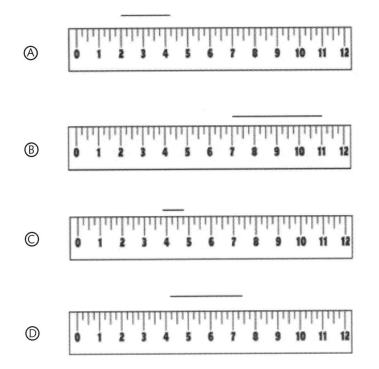

Day 1

Look at the pictures. Read the text and answer the questions. Reread the text to help you.

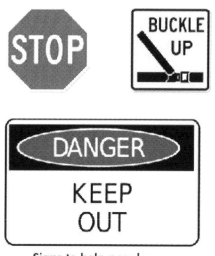

Signs to help people

You can see signs everywhere you go. Signs show and tell you about things and places. If you are on a trip, a sign might tell you how far the next town is or where an attraction is located. While in a town or on a street, you see signs for names of stores, businesses, and streets. You need to know that many signs tell us things to do and remember for our safety.

Some signs you know quickly. When you are riding in a car with your parents or others, you might see the stop sign. It is easily recognized. The word stop is in bold and the sign background is red. If you see this sign, be sure to stop. If you are walking look both ways to check to see if anything is coming before you go on.

Another sign that is important in traveling is the buckle up seat belt sign. Many states have this on their highways to remind people that not only it is the law to buckle up, but it is for safety, too. Seat belts keep you from getting hurt in case you are in an accident. Buckle up every time you get in a vehicle.

The third sign shown, you might not notice, but it is very important whether you are walking along with a friend or riding in a vehicle. If you see the DANGER sign, it means that you must not go near that place. It might mean that the place or building has chemicals or materials that are harmful. You need to stay away because there is a threat that you could be hurt.

Signs are important in our lives and can help us know where to go, what to do, and what to stay away from, too.

5. What point is the author trying to make in this selection? Mark the best answer.

Ⓐ   The point the author is trying to make is that signs are everywhere.
Ⓑ   The point the author is trying to make is that signs are important to learn and follow.
Ⓒ   The point the author is trying to make is to buckle up.
Ⓓ   The point the author is trying to make is that signs are on streets.

6. Fill in the T-chart to show what the reasons are that support the point of the text.

	Danger signs tell you to stay away from something.	Seat belt signs tell you to put on your seat belt.	Stop signs tell you to stop.
Stop Sign	☐	☐	☐
Buckle up sign.	☐	☐	☐
Danger Sign	☐	☐	☐

7. Which 2 are NOT reasons for following signs?

Ⓐ Signs are hard to figure out.
Ⓑ Only adults need to learn signs.
Ⓒ Signs help keep you safe.
Ⓓ Signs show you what to and what not to do.

8. Using the author's point and reasons, write why signs are important. Reread the text for help

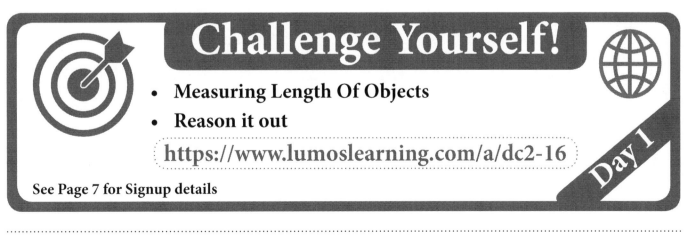

Challenge Yourself!

• **Measuring Length Of Objects**

• **Reason it out**

https://www.lumoslearning.com/a/dc2-16

Day 1

See Page 7 for Signup details

Measure Length Of Object Using Two Different Length Units (2.MD.A.2)

1. Look at the ruler below, then choose the true statement.

Ⓐ 2 inches is equivalent to 2 centimeters.
Ⓑ Inches are shorter than centimeters.
Ⓒ 7 centimeters is less than 3 inches.
Ⓓ 12 centimeters is closer to 6 inches than 5 inches.

2. Look at the ruler below, then choose the true statement.

Ⓐ 3 inches is between 7 and 8 centimeters.
Ⓑ There are 12 centimeters in 4 inches.
Ⓒ 8 centimeters is less than 3 inches.
Ⓓ 5 inches is longer than 13 centimeters.

3. Look at the ruler below, then choose the statement that is NOT true.

Ⓐ 1 inch is between 2 and 3 centimeters.
Ⓑ 7 centimeters is less than 3 inches.
Ⓒ 10 centimeters are less than 4 inches.
Ⓓ 2 ½ inches is more than 7 centimeters.

4. Look at the ruler below, then choose the statement that is NOT true.

Ⓐ 1 centimeter is less than ½ an inch.
Ⓑ 7 centimeters is closer to 2 inches than 3 inches.
Ⓒ 5 inches is less than 13 centimeters.
Ⓓ 2 inches is closer to 5 centimeters than 6 centimeters.

Compare and contrast (RI.8.4)

Day 2

Do You Know Cats?

Cats are very interesting! Many people have them as pets.
Here are a few neat facts you might not know about cats.

1. Cats like to sleep most of the time. (about 12 hours a day)
2. They can jump up to 7x as long as they are.
3. Their tongues are like sandpaper.
4. Cats can make over 100 different kinds of noises.
5. When put their paws in and out, they are happy.
6. A grown-up cat has 30 teeth.
7. They can jump from high places and still be ok.
8. They say hello to other cats by touching noses.
9. They cannot see if it is totally dark.
10. Cats can run very fast.
11. Their sense of hearing is excellent.
12. Calico cats are usually girl cats.
13. Baby cats are called kittens, grown boy cats are called Toms, and grown girl cats can be called Queens.

Cat Facts

I read an article on important things we need to know about cats. Here are some of those things.

1. Cats can be sad.
2. Cats cannot see in the dark like some people think. They need to have a little bit of light to see
3. Cats can hear very well, but not as good as dogs.
4. They have 20 bones in their tails.
5. Cats say hi to each other by touching their noses to each other.
6. Cats can be right or left handed. Most cats do use their right paw more.
7. Cats that live with people usually live to be 12 yrs old.
8. Cats take baths by licking themselves.
9. Domestic cats (those that live with people) love to play.

10. There are about 500 kinds of domestic cats.
11. Kittens are born with blue eyes and then most change colors.
12. Cats have 4 legs, 5 toes on each front paw, only 4 on back paws.
13. They sleep most of the day.

5. What does this article talk mostly about? Mark the best answer that supports it.

Ⓐ Cats sleep most of the time.
Ⓑ Calico cats are usually girl cats.
Ⓒ There are many interesting facts about cats.
Ⓓ Cats can jump high.

6. What sense of hearing do cats have? Mark the best answer.

Ⓐ Their sense of hearing is 7x better than ours.
Ⓑ They have a very good sense of hearing.
Ⓒ They cannot hear very well.
Ⓓ It does not tell about their sense of hearing.

7. List the different names the text says cats can be called.

| |
| |
| |

8. Are cats left or right handed? Write your own sentence. Use a fact from the list to help you.

| |
| |
| |

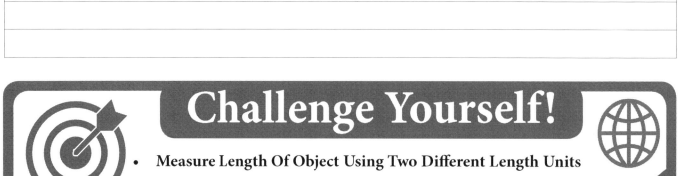

Challenge Yourself!

- Measure Length Of Object Using Two Different Length Units
- Compare and contrast

https://www.lumoslearning.com/a/dc2-17

Day 2

See Page 7 for Signup details

Day 3

1. The height of an orange is about 8 ___?

Ⓐ Centimeters
Ⓑ Feet
Ⓒ Inches
Ⓓ Meters

2. The length of a fork is about 6 _____ ?

Ⓐ Centimeters
Ⓑ Feet
Ⓒ Inches
Ⓓ Meters

3. The height of a door is about 7 ___?

Ⓐ Centimeters
Ⓑ Feet
Ⓒ Inches
Ⓓ Meters

4. The length of a paper clip is about 12 ___?

Ⓐ Centimeters
Ⓑ Feet
Ⓒ Inches
Ⓓ Meters

5. Read the list of words below. When we look at words, we can put them in order of the alphabet to help understand and read them. This list can be done by the first letter. Write the words in the correct ABC order.

(A) banana
(B) drive
(C) apple
(D) carrot
(E) elephant

1	
2	
3	
4	
5	

6. We can also sort words by their second letter if the first letter is the same. Look at the list below. Mark the long vowel word that is NOT in the correct ABC order.

(A) Tail
(B) Train
(C) Team
(D) Tone

7. When 2 vowels are together in a word, the first vowel is usually long and the second one silent. Read the list of words in the box and mark which has a short vowel sound, and which has a long vowel sound

	Short vowel sound	Long vowel sound
Mail	☐	☐
Street	☐	☐
Bat	☐	☐
Box	☐	☐

8. Read the words below and write the vowel combination for each.

	Vowel Combination
sneak	
goat	
trail	
clean	
deep	

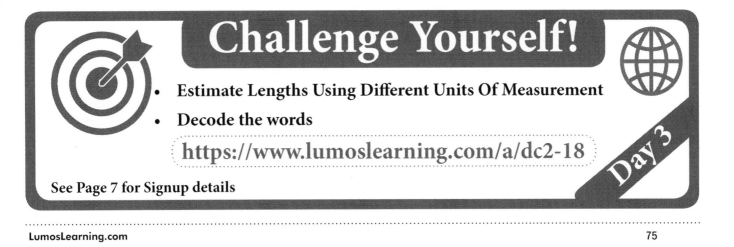

Challenge Yourself!

- Estimate Lengths Using Different Units Of Measurement
- Decode the words

https://www.lumoslearning.com/a/dc2-18

Day 3

See Page 7 for Signup details

Compare The Length Of Objects (2.MD.A.4)

1. How much longer is Rectangle A than Rectangle B?

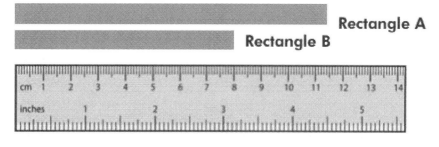

Ⓐ 3 ½ inches
Ⓑ 4 centimeters
Ⓒ 4 inches
Ⓓ 3 ½ centimeters

2. How much shorter is Rectangle A than Rectangle B?

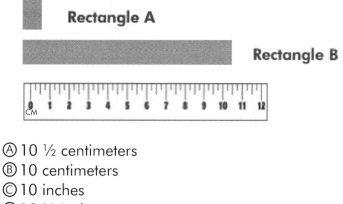

Ⓐ 10 ½ centimeters
Ⓑ 10 centimeters
Ⓒ 10 inches
Ⓓ 10 ½ inches

3. How much longer is Rectangle B than Rectangle A?

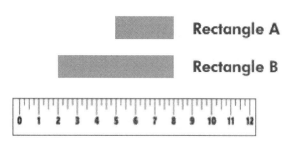

Ⓐ The rectangles are the same length.
Ⓑ 3 inches
Ⓒ 5 inches
Ⓓ 2 inches

4. How much longer is Rectangle A than Rectangle B?

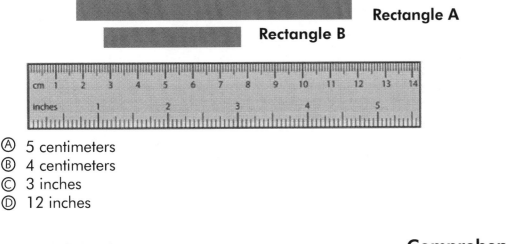

Rectangle A

Rectangle B

Ⓐ 5 centimeters
Ⓑ 4 centimeters
Ⓒ 3 inches
Ⓓ 12 inches

Day 4

A giraffe is a very tall animal. They can be found in the wild in Africa. Many zoos have giraffes, too. When we think of or picture a giraffe, we see the long, long neck. They are extremely tall. It would take at about 3 humans to be as tall as a giraffe. By being this tall, they can keep a close eye out for any animals that could hurt them, like hyenas or lions.

They weigh over 2 thousand pounds and can run about 35 miles an hour.
A funny thing is that the male is called a bull and the female is called a cow.

Giraffes are plant eating animals. They eat leaves and tiny branches called twigs. Giraffes do not drink much water. The reason for this is that they get most of their water from the leaves they eat. 75% of the time, giraffes are eating or roaming around. They even sleep standing up.

5. Which 3 of the following are facts about giraffes that you read in the story?

Ⓐ   Giraffes weigh over 2 thousand pounds.
Ⓑ   Giraffes sleep most of the day.
Ⓒ   Giraffes sleep standing up.
Ⓓ   Giraffes can be found in the wild in Africa.

6. Find the correct sentence about how fast giraffes can run. Mark your answer.

Ⓐ   They can run over 75 miles an hour
Ⓑ   They can run about 35 miles an hour.
Ⓒ   They do not run, they jump.
Ⓓ   They run about 10 miles an hour.

7. Why don't giraffes drink a lot of water like other animals? Write your own sentence.

8. Look at the chart. Mark if the detail is or is not a fact about giraffes.

	Is a fact	Is not a fact
Giraffes eat mice.	☐	☐
Giraffes can be 3 times taller than people.	☐	☐
Giraffes are only found in Africa.	☐	☐
Males are called bulls and females are called cows.	☐	☐

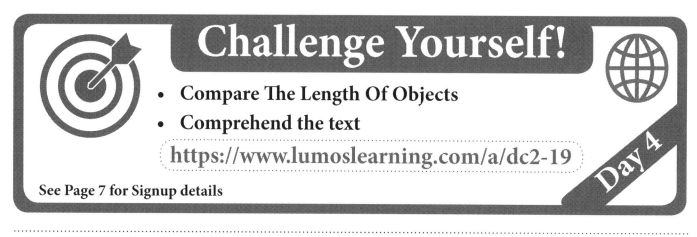

Challenge Yourself!

- Compare The Length Of Objects
- Comprehend the text

https://www.lumoslearning.com/a/dc2-19

Day 4

See Page 7 for Signup details

LumosLearning.com

Day 5

1. Brian had a piece of string that measures 36 inches. He cut the string and now the string is 12 inches. How much string did Brian cut?

   Ⓐ 12 inches
   Ⓑ 36 inches
   Ⓒ 24 inches
   Ⓓ 48 inches

2. The hallway from the cafeteria door to the office door is about 65 feet. From the office door to the gym door is about 30 feet. About how many feet is it from the cafeteria door to the gym door?

   Ⓐ About 95 feet
   Ⓑ About 30 feet
   Ⓒ About 35 feet
   Ⓓ About 65 feet

3. Lola cut 3 pieces of string all the same length in inches. The total length of all 3 pieces of string is 12 inches combined. What is the length of each piece of string?

   Ⓐ 12 inches
   Ⓑ 6 inches
   Ⓒ 3 inches
   Ⓓ 4 inches

4. Trevor's ink pen is 4 inches long. If he has 5 ink pens, what is the total length of all the pens if they were lined up?

   Ⓐ 9 inches
   Ⓑ 16 inches
   Ⓒ 20 inches
   Ⓓ 25 inches

Benjamin Franklin

Did you know that Benjamin Franklin was not only an inventor, but a scientist, soldier, politician, postmaster, and author? Benjamin Franklin was born in Boston, Massachusetts on January 17, 1706. He lived for 84 years. Franklin was one of our country's "Founding Fathers". He signed the Declaration of Independence, the Treaty of Paris and the U.S. Constitution. He is well known for his experiment with electricity, the kite and key with lightning during a thunderstorm. Franklin invented glasses called bifocals, too. Some of your grandparents may even have or remember his invention called the Franklin stove. One of his famous writings is Poor Richard's Almanac. It was written years ago and is still published and bought today. In this book, he gives facts about weather, and recipes. He wrote funny sayings and jokes in his works, too.

5. What did you learn from reading this story? Mark those that apply.

Ⓐ Benjamin Franklin was a Founding Father of our country.
Ⓑ Benjamin Franklin was an author and wrote Poor Richard's Almanac.
Ⓒ Benjamin Franklin was a skinny man with glasses.
Ⓓ He invented bifocals and the Franklin stove.

6. Fill in the words below to complete the sentences about Mr. Franklin.

U.S. Constitution
84
Founding Fathers
electricity

a. Franklin did experiments with a key, and kite during a thunderstorm to show

_____.

b. Benjamin Franklin is one of our country's _____.

c. He lived to be _____ years old.

d. Mr. Franklin signed the Declaration of Independence, the Treaty of Paris and the

_____.

7. List the 6 jobs that Mr. Franklin held as stated in the story.

8. What do you think the purpose of this text is? Write your own sentence.

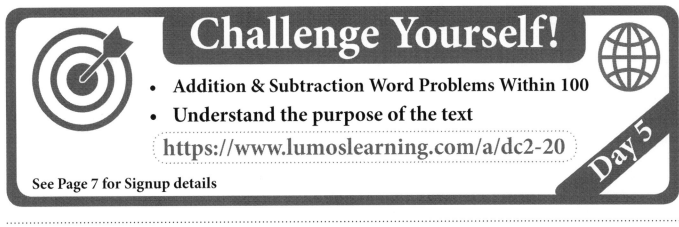

Challenge Yourself!

- Addition & Subtraction Word Problems Within 100
- Understand the purpose of the text

https://www.lumoslearning.com/a/dc2-20

Day 5

See Page 7 for Signup details

Swimming: 7 Tips to Become a Better Swimmer

Just about everyone knows how to swim, or at least play around in the water. But you want to be a competitive swimmer, so how do you set yourself apart from all those people who just want to hang out at the pool? Here's a guide on how to take it to the next level.

1. Make Time for Practice

The best swimmers spend the most amount of time in the pool practicing their technique. While natural ability gives some people an advantage, the great ones are the ones who keep practicing.

Set aside time each day for some sort of swimming activity or exercise that you can do. Even if you don't have access to a pool every day, there's tons of exercises and drills that you can do to build strength and endurance. Make a plan and stick to it.

2. Know Your Sport

Freestyle swimming is the most common and well-known forms of swimming. A stroke is the full circle motion your arm makes when swimming. A freestyle stroke can be broken down into four phases. Those phases are catch, pull, exit, and recovery.

The catch phase is when your hand goes out in front of you and hits the water. In the pull phase, your hand goes underwater and down toward the bottom of the pool. In this phase, you are "pulling" yourself through the water. The exit phase is when your hand is coming up from the bottom of the pull phase. Your hand comes up from the bottom and comes up beside your leg. In the recovery phase, your arm is out of the water and rotates back towards the catch.

3. Improve Each Phase of the Stroke

Try swimming with your hand closed during the catch and pull phases. This will increase your forearm strength and help improve your stroke.

During the exit phase, flick your wrist at the end before it comes out of the water.

During the recovery phase, focus on getting your hand and arm back in the water as quickly as possible. The longer your hand is out of the water, the less time you spend pulling yourself forward.

4. Build Your Strength

To improve your swimming ability, you will need to improve your strength. Body weight exercises can be done anywhere and aren't likely to cause injury like weight lifting can.

Exercises like pushups and pull-ups strengthen your upper body. Doing these exercises will help you when you are pulling through the water.

Lunges, squats, and calf raises strengthen your lower body. These exercises will help you when you are kicking your legs, giving you more speed through the water.

Core exercises focus on your stomach, sides, lower back, and hips. Exercises such as crunches, leg raises, and bicycle kicks give your core a great workout. Strengthening your core will help you keep great form throughout your swim.

5. Increase Your Endurance

Even when you aren't in the pool, you can keep active to improve your endurance. Endurance exercises like biking and running help build your lung capacity so you can swim longer. Sprinting will help build muscle endurance so you can swim faster and harder without getting tired.

6. Breathing

It is important to learn to breathe correctly when swimming. New swimmers have a habit of bringing their head out of the water and breathing through their mouth.

Instead of bringing your head all the way out of the water, take breaths through your nose as you turn your head to the side. Practice this technique in shallow water without swimming, then try it while swimming.

7. Find a Good Coach.

Even the most successful athletes have coaches. A good coach can set you up with an exercise program. The coach also gets to see you swim on a regular basis. That way she can tell you what you might be doing wrong and help correct it.
And most importantly, remember to have fun!

This Week's Online Activities

- **Reading Assignment**
- **Vocabulary Practice**
- **Write Your Summer Diary**

https://www.lumoslearning.com/a/slh2-3

See Page 7 for Signup details

Weekly Fun Summer Photo Contest

Take a picture of your summer fun activity and share it on Twitter or Instagram

Use the **#SummerLearning** mention

@LumosLearning on Twitter or

@lumos.learning on Instagram

Tag friends and increase your chances of winning the contest

Participate and stand a chance to WIN $50 Amazon gift card!

Represent Whole Numbers As Lengths On A Number Line (2.MD.B.6)

1. 54 + ___ = 74

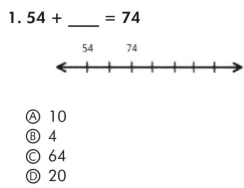

   Ⓐ 10
   Ⓑ 4
   Ⓒ 64
   Ⓓ 20

2. If you start at 15 and jump three times, what number will you land on?

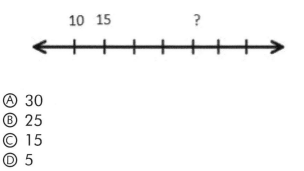

   Ⓐ 30
   Ⓑ 25
   Ⓒ 15
   Ⓓ 5

3. How many times will you jump to show 22 + 6?

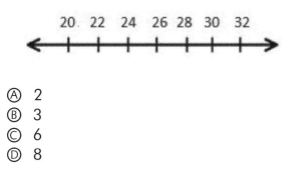

   Ⓐ 2
   Ⓑ 3
   Ⓒ 6
   Ⓓ 8

4. How many times will you jump to get from 35 to 45?

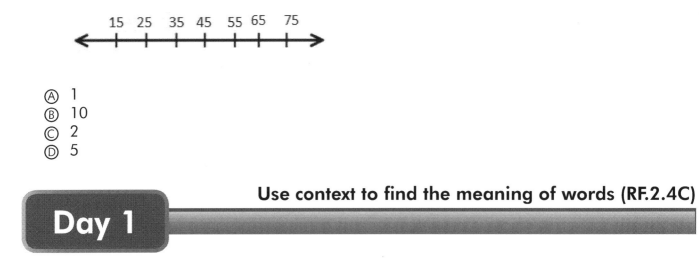

   Ⓐ 1
   Ⓑ 10
   Ⓒ 2
   Ⓓ 5

Day 1

Use context to find the meaning of words (RF.2.4C)

Read the text below. Reread it at least three times to help you. The words in bold may be new words for you. To use context clues in a text, it is important to read all the sentences around the new word. This will help you understand the meaning of the new words. After you have read the text many times, use what you learn to answer the questions about the new vocabulary.

Regional temperatures are changing with the climate. This change in certain areas of the country makes it hard for plants and animals to live. Animals may need to relocate to places that have the temperatures they are used to living in. This move can be difficult for them. This change may cause some **species** to move farther north where the weather is cooler or farther south where the weather is warmer. Many kinds of animals migrate each year and more are doing so with the climate changes. With the changes in climate, there may be different places in which plants can still grow in certain areas. The land and water are also affected. Researchers use data to help them understand these changes. Reports, charts, graphs, and daily monitoring of land is detailed in the information gathered. Currents in the oceans have impact on the climate changes, too. The speed and direction of the water moving on the ocean floor is being studied to help add more information. Scientists hope this research will help them understand more about climate change.

5. Which is the best definition of the word "Regional"?

   Ⓐ Cities in the country
   Ⓑ Certain areas of the country
   Ⓒ A way to get data for the scientists
   Ⓓ Climate change

6. Why do animals relocate? Write a sentence that explains.

7. Highlight the set of under lined words that help you in understanding the word "species".

This change may cause some species to move farther north where the <u>weather is cooler or farther</u> south where the weather is warmer. <u>Many kinds of animals</u> migrate each year and more are doing so with the <u>climate changes</u>.

8. List what scientists use in their "data".

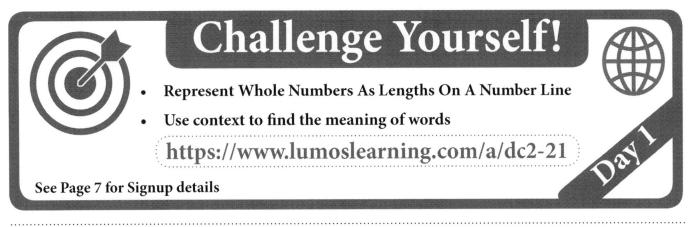

Challenge Yourself!

• Represent Whole Numbers As Lengths On A Number Line

• Use context to find the meaning of words

https://www.lumoslearning.com/a/dc2-21

Day 1

See Page 7 for Signup details

Tell And Write Time From Clocks (2.MD.C.7)

1. What time is shown on the clock below?

Ⓐ 5:05
Ⓑ 6:01
Ⓒ 1:06
Ⓓ 6:05

2. What time is shown on the clock below?

Ⓐ 11:15
Ⓑ 3:55
Ⓒ 11:03
Ⓓ 11:20

3. What time is shown on the clock below?

Ⓐ 9:30
Ⓑ 8:06
Ⓒ 8:30
Ⓓ 8:15

4. Mark has basketball practice at the time that is shown on the clock. What time does Mark have basketball practice.

Ⓐ 4:45
Ⓑ 4:00
Ⓒ 3:45
Ⓓ 3:09

People, Places, and Things (L.2.1A)

Day 2

5. Collective nouns show a group of things. Read the sentences below and choose the collective noun in each sentence. Highlight the collective noun.

Ⓐ We saw a flock of geese in the sky.
Ⓑ Mama said that our cat had a litter of kittens.
Ⓒ Buzzing around us was a swarm of bees.
Ⓓ The pack of wolves howled in the night.

6. Read the list of collective nouns and choose the right one for each group to describe it.

Ⓐ flock
Ⓑ bunch
Ⓒ swarm
Ⓓ herd

Group	Collective Noun
Cows	
Bananas	
birds	
flies	

7. Mark the sentences that have collective nouns in them.

Ⓐ We looked for the deck of cards.
Ⓑ Sara picked up the wash.
Ⓒ The children were playing on the playground.
Ⓓ There was a colony of ants in our garden.

8. Which of the following phrases does NOT have a collective noun in it? Mark your answer.

Ⓐ ran to the store
Ⓑ band of soldiers
Ⓒ bundle of papers
Ⓓ bunch of grapes

Challenge Yourself!

- Tell And Write Time From Clocks
- People, Places, and Things

https://www.lumoslearning.com/a/dc2-22

Day 2

See Page 7 for Signup details

Day 3

1. How much money in all is 1 dollar, 3 dimes, and 4 pennies?

    Ⓐ $1.19
    Ⓑ $1.79
    Ⓒ $1.30
    Ⓓ $1.34

2. What is the value of 2 quarters, 3 dimes, 4 nickels, and 1 penny?

    Ⓐ $1.01
    Ⓑ $2.01
    Ⓒ $0.91
    Ⓓ $1.41

3. What is the value of 3 dollars, 4 quarters, and 6 pennies?

    Ⓐ $4.46
    Ⓑ $3.46
    Ⓒ $4.06
    Ⓓ $3.64

4. Billy has 6 quarters, 3 dimes, and 2 nickels. How much money does Billy have in all?

    Ⓐ $1.80
    Ⓑ $1.90
    Ⓒ $2.80
    Ⓓ $2.90

5. Read the words below and mark the right boxes.

little elephant
really walking
quickly running
fuzzy slipper

	Noun	Adjective	Verb	Adverb
little				
elephant				
really				
walking				
quickly				
running				
fuzzy				
slipper				

6. Read each group of words below. A complete sentence must have a subject and predicate. The subject has the noun in it. The predicate has the verb in it. Mark the 2 sentences that are complete and make sense.

Ⓐ   Fishing near the lake.
Ⓑ   Margie and I love to go hiking in the woods.
Ⓒ   Tracy is happy that he has a new little baby brother.
Ⓓ   Skipping down the sidewalk while it is raining.

7. Read the phrase below. Decide what part of the sentence is missing. Write your answers in the blank. The sentence is missing a subject or predicate.

ran a long way home	
My friends and I	
Grandma and Grandpa	
skipping in the rain	

8. Write the right verb for each sentence below. Be careful, each word can only be used one time.(ran, follow, bake, see, draw)

a. We like to .... pictures in Art Class.

b. She would not .... the directions the teacher told us.

c. I .... all the way home when I was late for dinner.

d. Grandma will .... my favorite birthday cake!

e. Did you .... her look of surprise?

Challenge Yourself!

- **Solve Word Problems Involving Money**
- **Language conventions**

https://www.lumoslearning.com/a/dc2-23

Day 3

See Page 7 for Signup details

Day 4

The measurement of Kim's pieces of ribbon are plotted on the line plot. Use the line plot below to answer all the questions.

Note: Each x represents 2 pieces of ribbon

INCHES OF RIBBON

1. What lengths does none of Kim's ribbons measure?

Ⓐ 1 inch and 2 inches
Ⓑ 4 inches and 5 inches
Ⓒ 4 inches and 6 inches
Ⓓ 2 inches and 7 inches

2. How many pieces of ribbon does Kim have that is 7 inches?

Ⓐ 2
Ⓑ 1
Ⓒ 3
Ⓓ 0

3. How many pieces of Kim's ribbon is only 1 inch long?

Ⓐ 4
Ⓑ 2
Ⓒ 8
Ⓓ 6

4. Kim can only use the ribbon that is 3 or more inches. How many pieces of ribbon can Kim use?

Ⓐ 5
Ⓑ 10
Ⓒ 4
Ⓓ 12

5. When there is more of one thing, some words need an "s" added to them. Examples: tree becomes trees, plane becomes planes. Singular means one and plural means more than one.

Some words must be changed to become plural.

If a noun ends in "lf", you change the "f" to a "v" and add "es".

Change the words from singular to plural.

wolf	
shelf	
leaf	
knife	
elf	

6. To make words ending in a "y" to plural, you change the "y" to "I" and add "es". Read the list of words below and make them plural.

butterfly	
fly	
story	
baby	

7. To make some words plural you add "es". Make the singular words match the plurals in the table below.

potato	
tomato	
wish	
bench	
box	

8. Sometimes when a noun becomes plural, the word changes all together. Read the sentences below. The underlined word is singular and should be plural. Mark the correct plural noun.

a. She was afraid of <u>mouse</u>.

Ⓐ mouses
Ⓑ mice

b. All the <u>person</u> were happy!

Ⓐ people
Ⓑ peoples

c. I heard so many <u>goose</u> honking at the park.

Ⓐ geeses
Ⓑ geese

d. Her <u>foot</u> had grown, and her shoes did not fit.

Ⓐ foots
Ⓑ feet

Challenge Yourself!

- **Generate Measurement Data**
- **Regular and Irregular Plural Nouns**

https://www.lumoslearning.com/a/dc2-24

See Page 7 for Signup details

Day 4

Day 5

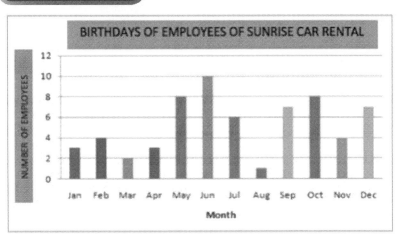

Use the bar graph to answer all the questions.

1. Which month had the fewest number of employee birthdays?

Ⓐ August
Ⓑ June
Ⓒ March
Ⓓ January

2. How many employees have a birthday in January?

Ⓐ 2
Ⓑ 4
Ⓒ 2 ½
Ⓓ 3

3. Which month had the most employee birthdays?

Ⓐ May
Ⓑ June
Ⓒ August
Ⓓ March

4. If Sunrise Car Rental gets a new employee that has a birthday in December, how many employees will have December birthdays?

Ⓐ 7
Ⓑ 8
Ⓒ 9
Ⓓ 6

Reflexive pronouns (L.2.1C)

Reflexive pronouns tell about the subject. Example: herself, myself, ourselves, himself, themselves, yourself.

5. Read the sentences and highlight the reflexive pronoun in each sentence.

The children helped themselves to bake.

I see myself as a ballerina.

Maggy knows how to sew by herself.

We tell ourselves to be nice to each other

6. Read the sentences and decide what is the subject and what is the reflexive pronoun in each one.

1. **I did it myself.**
2. **She made herself a cake.**
3. **We ran by ourselves to the park.**

Subject	Reflexive pronoun

7. Choose the right reflexive pronoun for each sentence. Write it in the blank.

a. We understood the directions by _____.
   (themselves, ourselves)

b. She watched the baby by _____.
   (herself, himself)

c. They cannot do it _____.
   (ourselves, themselves)

d. He made the kite _____.
   (herself, himself)

8. Which of the following sentences does NOT have a reflexive pronoun in it?

Ⓐ Mark ran the mile by himself.
Ⓑ Sarah and Tammy played the piano.
Ⓒ Tyrone caught himself a huge fish.
Ⓓ They made pies themselves.

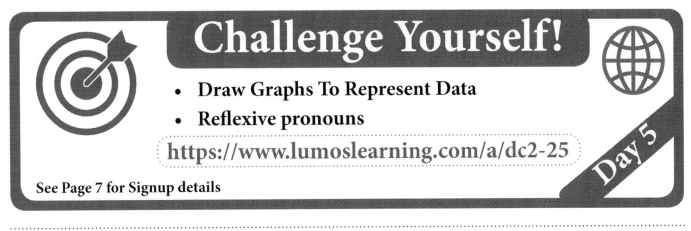

Challenge Yourself!

- **Draw Graphs To Represent Data**
- **Reflexive pronouns**

https://www.lumoslearning.com/a/dc2-25

Day 5

See Page 7 for Signup details

Maze Game

MAZE GAME

Help Santa Claus find the Christmas tree

MAZE GAME

Help fox find mushroom

MAZE GAME

Help rabbit find carrot

MAZE GAME

Help squirrel find acorn

This Week's Online Activities

- **Reading Assignment**
- **Vocabulary Practice**
- **Write Your Summer Diary**

https://www.lumoslearning.com/a/slh2-3

See Page 7 for Signup details

Weekly Fun Summer Photo Contest

📷 Take a picture of your summer fun activity and share it on Twitter or Instagram

Use the **#SummerLearning** mention

@LumosLearning on Twitter 🐦 or

@lumos.learning on Instagram 📷

🔗 Tag friends and increase your chances of winning the contest

Participate and stand a chance to WIN $50 Amazon gift card!

Day 1

Recognize And Draw Shapes (2.G.A.1)

1. Which shape is shown below?

- Ⓐ Square
- Ⓑ Rhombus
- Ⓒ Rectangle
- Ⓓ Triangle

2. Which shape has four equal sides?

- Ⓐ Rectangle
- Ⓑ Square
- Ⓒ Hexagon
- Ⓓ Triangle

3. Which shape is the face of a cube?

- Ⓐ Triangle
- Ⓑ Square
- Ⓒ Rectangle
- Ⓓ Circle

4. Which shape is shown below?

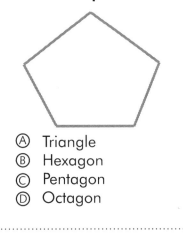

- Ⓐ Triangle
- Ⓑ Hexagon
- Ⓒ Pentagon
- Ⓓ Octagon

Verbs tell the action in a sentence. They are a part of the predicate. Some verbs can be changed from what is happening now (present tense) to what happened before (past tense). Most verbs are changed from present to past by adding an "ed". But some do not follow that rule. An irregular past tense verb is one where either the verb is changed to a new word or stays the same in present and past tense.

5. What do verbs do in a sentence? Mark the 2 best answers.

Ⓐ Verbs name the noun in the sentence.
Ⓑ Verbs tell the action in a sentence.
Ⓒ Verbs are words in a sentence that tell about the subject.
Ⓓ Verbs are part of the predicate.

6. Fill in the blank to answer the sentence about irregular verbs. Use what you read to help you.

An irregular past tense verb is one where either ....

....

7. Below is a list of present and past tense verbs. Mark the irregular verbs that tell what has already happened (past tense).

Ⓐ sat
Ⓑ hide
Ⓒ tell
Ⓓ ate
Ⓔ sit
Ⓕ hid
Ⓖ told
Ⓗ eat

8. Read the sentences and pick the correct irregular past tense verb to answer each one.

    a. Yesterday we _____ to the bus.
       (run, ran)

    b. Last Saturday, Mary _____ shopping with her mother.
       (went, go)

    c. They _____ the deer when they went on vacation a month ago.
       (saw, see)

    d. When I was in first grade, Mr. Samuel _____ me how to read.
       (teach, taught)

Challenge Yourself!

- **Recognize And Draw Shapes**
- **Past tense of verbs**

https://www.lumoslearning.com/a/dc2-26

See Page 7 for Signup details

Day 1

Partition a Rectangle Into Rows And Columns (2.G.A.2)

1. Which shape is portioned into 3 rows and 4 columns?

Ⓐ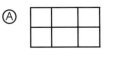

Ⓑ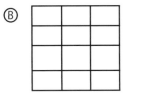

Ⓒ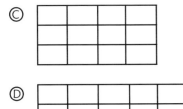

Ⓓ

2. Which shape is portioned into 4 columns and 5 rows?

Ⓐ

Ⓑ

Ⓒ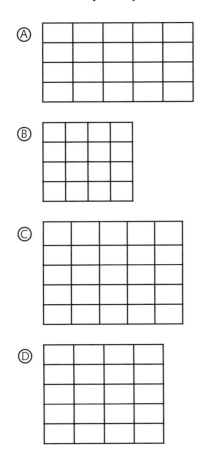

Ⓓ

3. How many rows and columns are in the shape below?

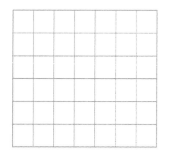

Ⓐ 5 rows, 5 columns
Ⓑ 4 rows, 5 columns
Ⓒ 6 rows, 6 columns
Ⓓ 4 columns, 5 rows

4. How many rows and columns are in the shape below?

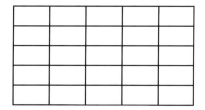

Ⓐ 6 rows, 6 columns
Ⓑ 7 rows, 6 columns
Ⓒ 6 rows, 7 columns
Ⓓ 7 rows, 7 columns

Day 2

Simple and compound sentences (L.2.1F)

Sentences must have a subject (noun and any describing words) and predicate (verb and any helping words) to be complete. If words put together do not have both a subject and a verb they do not make a sentence. These words are phrases.

5. Let's look at the story below. Some of the words are not in a complete sentence. Highlight the words (phrases) that are not a complete sentence.

Mary and Jane want. to go to the store. They got ready. Mary asked her mother. for some money. Her mother gave her $2. Jane got $5 from her dad.

5.1 Make the phrases that were not complete sentences, complete by putting them together. Be sure to take out the period and join the words. Write them below.

[ ]

6. Write the 3 complete sentences from the story. Reread the story.

Mary and Jane want. to go to the store. They got ready. Mary asked her mother. for some money. Her mother gave her $2. Jane got $5 from her dad.

[ ]

7. Read the phrases below. Fill the subject to the boxes to make the sentence complete.

Roberto and Miguel

The beautiful ponies

She

The chicken soup

Subject	Predicate
	were fun to ride.
	love to play football.
	was good to eat.
	brushed her hair.

8. **Read the predicates and match them with the correct subjects. Use each one only one time to make the best sentences.**

Betty
The race car
The dish
The alarm

Predicate	Subject
sped down the hill.	
broke as it fell to the floor.	
started ringing when the fire began.	
rode her bike up the road.	

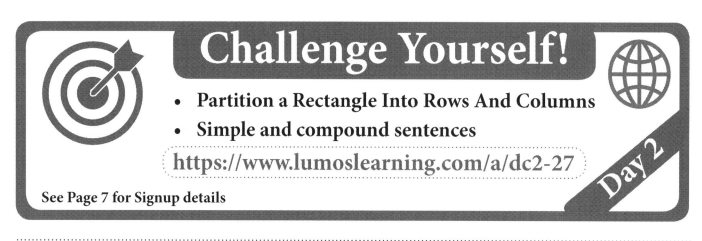

Challenge Yourself!

• Partition a Rectangle Into Rows And Columns
• Simple and compound sentences

https://www.lumoslearning.com/a/dc2-27

Day 2

See Page 7 for Signup details

Partition Circles And Rectangles (2.G.A.3)

1. Which shape is portioned into two halves?

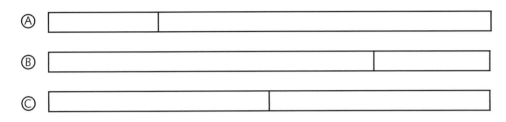

Ⓐ

Ⓑ

Ⓒ

2. Which shape is portioned into thirds?

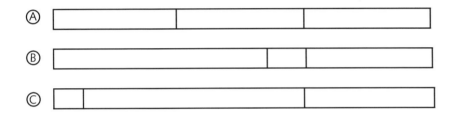

Ⓐ

Ⓑ

Ⓒ

3. Which shape is portioned into fourths?

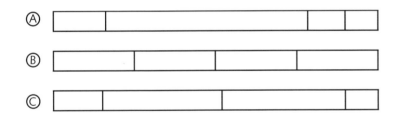

Ⓐ

Ⓑ

Ⓒ

4. What choice best describes the shaded part below?

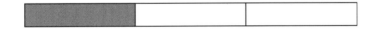

Ⓐ One-Third
Ⓑ One-Fourth
Ⓒ One-Half

Day 3

5. Highlight the proper nouns in the sentences below.

The little puppy made Sarah very happy.
They went to see the show in Dallas Texas
If you love candy,you will love Valentine's Day!
John and Skipper played ball on Saturday.

6. The names of products are capitalized, too. An example is Cheetos. It names the snack. If you had the word chips, it would not be capitalized. It did not tell the product name of chips. Read the list in the box. Mark the ones that name or do not name a particular product.

	Names a particular product	**Does not name a particular product**
Cheerios cereal		
popcorn		
Skippy peanut butter		
Kraft cheese		

7. We know that a comma is used in a list of words, and to join clauses in sentences. Commas are also used in the headings and closings of letters. For example- Dear Mom, is an example of how to use a comma when you start a letter. For the closing of a letter here is an example- Yours truly, - then your name would go on the next line.

Read the list and Mark the ones that use a comma correctly.

Ⓐ Dear Mayor,
Ⓑ Thank, you
Ⓒ Dearest Grandma,
Ⓓ Respectfully,

8. The apostrophe mark ' is used to combine two words into one word to make a contraction. If the word "not" is the second word in the sentence, take out the letter "o", put in the ' and make the contraction. Read the list of words and make them into contractions. Write the new word.

a. should not = _____

b. is not = _____

c. did not = _____

Challenge Yourself!

• Partition Circles And Rectangles
• Understand Language conventions

https://www.lumoslearning.com/a/dc2-28

Day 3

See Page 7 for Signup details

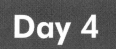

Day 4

1. Jimmy exercised for 36 minutes on Monday. He exercised for 12 more minutes on Tuesday, than he did on Monday. How many minutes did Jimmy exercise in all for both Monday and Tuesday?

   Ⓐ 48
   Ⓑ 24
   Ⓒ 38
   Ⓓ 84

2. Mark earned a 98 on his Math quiz this week. He earned 11 points higher this week than he earned on his quiz last week. What grade did Mark earn on last week's quiz?

3. Put a check mark under the correct equation to solve each word problem.

	34+17=?	34-17=?
Lisa had 34 books. She read 17. How many books did she not read?		
Lisa bought 17 books. She had 34. How many books does Lisa have now?		

4. Brittney and Joshua are saving their money to buy a new video game for $59. Brittney has $26 saved and Joshua has $19 saved. Answer below questions.

How much money have Brittney and Joshua saved altogether?	
How much more money does Brittney have saved than Joshua?	
How much more money do they need to save to buy the video game?	

5. Remember that holidays are always capitalized. Read the list of words and mark the holidays.

   Ⓐ Easter
   Ⓑ Eggs
   Ⓒ Memorial Day
   Ⓓ Valentine's Day
   Ⓔ Presents

6. Read the sentences below. Mark the one that uses capitalization correctly for holidays.

   Ⓐ The family went on a vacation for the fourth of July
   Ⓑ Mary and her mother made cupcakes for Veteran's Day.
   Ⓒ The team rode in a parade on president's day.
   Ⓓ Grandpa does not like halloween.

7. Names of products are capitalized, too. Examples of these are Cheerios for a cereal, and Kraft for cheese or milk products. If an exact name is not there, do not capitalize it. Read the words in the box and mark if they should be capitalized

	Capitalize	Do not capitalize
Ford		
Truck		
Amazon		
Dog food		
M & M's		
Candy		
Store		
Coca Cola		

8. Read the sentences below. Mark the 2 that use product names correctly.

Ⓐ Most people like to eat Lay's chips.
Ⓑ He drove a bright shiny Toyota truck.
Ⓒ The dentist says to use crest toothpaste.
Ⓓ We feed our dog purina dog chow.

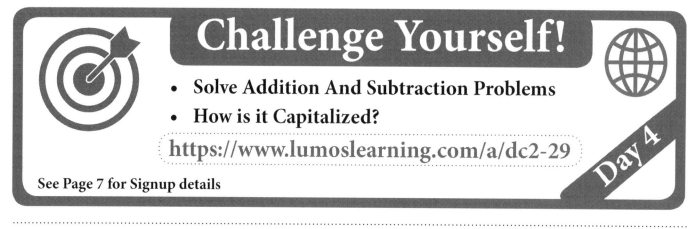

Challenge Yourself!

- **Solve Addition And Subtraction Problems**
- **How is it Capitalized?**

https://www.lumoslearning.com/a/dc2-29

See Page 7 for Signup details

Day 4

Day 5

1. Select all of the equations that have a difference of 4.

Ⓐ 17 - 4 = ?

Ⓑ 12 - 8 = ?

Ⓒ 19 - 15 = ?

Ⓓ 20 - 5 = ?

Ⓔ 10 - 6 = ?

2. What number added to itself equals 14?

3. Place a check mark under the correct column to tell whether the equation equals 12 or does not equal 12.

	Equals 12	Does not Equal 12
14 + 3=?		
11 + 1=?		
20 - 8=?		
18 - 6=?		
2 + 10=?		

4. Complete the table by filling in the missing number in each equation.

15	+		=	17
19	-	7	=	
	+	5	=	7
18	-		=	3

5. **Commas are used in greetings of letters and closings.**
   Choose the answers that are correct use of a comma in the greeting of a letter.

   Ⓐ Dear Calvin,
   Ⓑ Dearest Aunt Sue
   Ⓒ Dearest Grandmother
   Ⓓ To Whom It May Concern,
   Ⓐ Dear William

6. **Read the letter. In both the start of a letter (salutation) and end of a letter (closing), a comma should be used at the end. Check and make the corrections if needed by adding a comma.**

   Dear Daddy

   I would like to thank you for the gift of a new bike. It is the best gift ever. I love the basket on the front and the bright red color of the seat.

   Thanks again

   L' Toya

7. Mark the correct answer that shows how to use a comma at the beginning of the letter.

Ⓐ Dear David
Ⓑ Dear Tabitha
Ⓒ Dear Franklin
Ⓓ Dear Aunt Bea,

8. Read the following salutations. Fix the ones that are not correct by rewriting them with a comma.

To the President

Dear Eddie

Dear Mom,

Hello Friend,

This Week's Online Activities

- Reading Assignment
- Vocabulary Practice
- Write Your Summer Diary

https://www.lumoslearning.com/a/slh2-3

See Page 7 for Signup details

Weekly Fun Summer Photo Contest

Take a picture of your summer fun activity and share it on Twitter or Instagram

Use the **#SummerLearning** mention

@LumosLearning on Twitter or

@lumos.learning on Instagram

Tag friends and increase your chances of winning the contest

Participate and stand a chance to WIN $50 Amazon gift card!

Groups Of Odd And Even Numbers (2.OA.C.3)

Day 1

1. Select all of the numbers that are even.

   Ⓐ 61
   Ⓑ 89
   Ⓒ 98
   Ⓓ 16
   Ⓔ 24

2. Choose all of the equations that will equal an odd number.

   Ⓐ 5+6=?
   Ⓑ 3+7=?
   Ⓒ 8+10=?
   Ⓓ 4+3=?
   Ⓔ 9+2=?

3. In her drawer, Carrie has 9 pairs of socks and 1 sock she could not find a match for. How many socks does Carrie have in her drawer?

4. Choose if each group of circle represents an even or odd number.

	EVEN	ODD
OOOOOOO OOOOOO		
OOOOOOOO OOOOOOOO		
OOOO + OOO = ?		
OO + OOOO = ?		

5. Contractions are made by joining two words into one word and leaving out a letter. You put an ' in place of the missing letter to make the contraction. Some kinds of contractions combine a word with the word "are". The letter "a" is then left out and the 'put in. Some kinds combine a word with the word "is". The letter "i" is left out and the ' put in.Read the first word and second word in each row and write contractions in the contraction column

First word	Second word	contraction
they	are	
we	are	
she	is	
he	is	
you	are	

6. Which 2 sentences have contractions in them? Mark them.

Ⓐ Jamie and I played in the park with our friends.
Ⓑ We aren't going to go shopping until Friday.
Ⓒ They're happy to go on vacation.
Ⓓ She ran home for supper.

7. Write the contractions with the words below using not as the second word. Remember to leave out the "o" in not and add an '.

    a. are = _____

    b. have = _____

    c. did = _____

    d. is = _____

8. **There are a couple of words that change completely when not is added as the second word and a contraction is made. Will not becomes won't and cannot becomes can't. Pick the sentence below that has one of these contractions in it. Mark your answer.**

Ⓐ Latifa can go into town with us.
Ⓑ The cows will eat their hay when it gets cold.
Ⓒ The firemen won't let the fire spread.
Ⓓ The police helped the lady cross the street

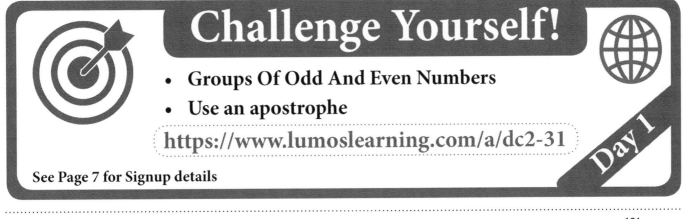

Challenge Yourself!

- **Groups Of Odd And Even Numbers**
- **Use an apostrophe**

https://www.lumoslearning.com/a/dc2-31

Day 1

See Page 7 for Signup details

Day 2

1. Select TWO equations that are represented by the array.

OOOOO
OOOOO
OOOOO

Ⓐ 5+5+5=?
Ⓑ 3×5=?
Ⓒ 3+3+3?
Ⓓ 3×3=?

2. Select TWO equations that are represented by the array.

OO
OO
OO
OO
OO

Ⓐ 5×2=?
Ⓑ 5+5+5+5+5=?
Ⓒ 2×2=?
Ⓓ 2+2+2+2+2=?

3. At band practice, there are 5 rows and 4 students in each row. How many students are at band practice?

4. Match each array to one of the sums by placing a check mark under the correct column.

	12	18
OOO OOO OOO OOO		
OOOOOOOOO OOOOOOOOO		
OOOO OOOO OOOO		
OOOOOO OOOOOO OOOOOO		

Day 2

5. Spelling has patterns in words that help us to remember how to spell them. Here is a pattern for spelling.

If a word has a short vowel sound and ends in the "k" sound, the "k" sound is spelled"ck".

Read the words below and Mark the ones that follow this rule.

Ⓐ Bike
Ⓑ Back
Ⓒ Rack
Ⓓ Stick
Ⓔ Flick
Ⓕ Brake
Ⓖ Like
Ⓗ Lake

6. If a word ends in the long "a" sound, the spelling pattern at the end is "ay". Choose YES or NO for each word in the box to show if the word follows this rule.

	Yes	No
play		
stay		
away		
bake		
story		

7. A spelling pattern for long e words is that the long "e" is usually spelled with "ee" or "ea" and sometimes "ie" when followed by the letter "c". Long e can also be spelled e in short words such as me, he, she be, and we. The word "the" is not usually long "e", but the "e" says "u" like in duck.

   Read the sentences below and Mark the long "e" spelled words. (Do not mark the word "the".) There can be more than one long "e" word in each sentence.

   Ⓐ We looked for the cat that ran up the tree.
   Ⓑ Sandra and I would like to eat a piece of chocolate cake.
   Ⓒ Please wash your hands.
   Ⓓ The ice will freeze in about an hour.

8. Read the words. Mark the ones that have the long "e" spelling.

   Ⓐ Better
   Ⓑ Beef
   Ⓒ Step
   Ⓓ Sleep
   Ⓔ Meat
   Ⓕ Met

Challenge Yourself!

• Addition Using Rectangular Arrays
• Spelling patterns

https://www.lumoslearning.com/a/dc2-32

Day 2

See Page 7 for Signup details

Day 3

1. **Choose a number that does not have any hundreds.**

   Ⓐ   300
   Ⓑ   58
   Ⓒ   700
   Ⓓ   900

2. **Choose a number that does not have any ones.**

   Ⓐ   809
   Ⓑ   340
   Ⓒ   209
   Ⓓ   33

3. **How many tens are bundled to make one hundred?**

4. **Place a check mark under each column of the correct number.**

	583	385	853	538
8 ones, 3 tens, 5 hundreds				
8 hundreds, 5 tens, 3 ones				
8 tens, 3 ones, 5 hundreds				
5 ones, 3 hundreds, 8 tens				

5. Dictionaries help you to spell, pronounce, and understand what words mean. The two guide words at the top of the pages show you if the word you want is on that page. The words on the page fall between the words in ABC order.

   If I wanted to check the spelling of the word - giraffe - which guide words would I use in a dictionary? Mark the best answer.

   Ⓐ dairy - doghouse
   Ⓑ germ - great
   Ⓒ gem - get
   Ⓓ fairy - fun

6. Read the sentence below. Then read the definitions for the words from a dictionary. Which word fits best in the sentence? Mark the answer.

   He was _____ to see his friends.

   Ⓐ Explosive - might become violent, dangerous
   Ⓑ Excited - eager, enthusiastic, anticipating emotions
   Ⓒ Skinny - narrow, slender, thin

7. Which 2 words need to be looked up in the dictionary to correct the spelling?

   Ⓐ happy
   Ⓑ forgeting
   Ⓒ childran
   Ⓓ complete

8. An online encyclopedia gives information about a topic. It can be used to help you write a report or understand more about something. Which 3 topics would you find the most information about in an online encyclopedia? Mark the ones that would help you research topics.

Ⓐ Funny
Ⓑ Rainforest
Ⓒ Trees
Ⓓ Walking
Ⓔ Cats

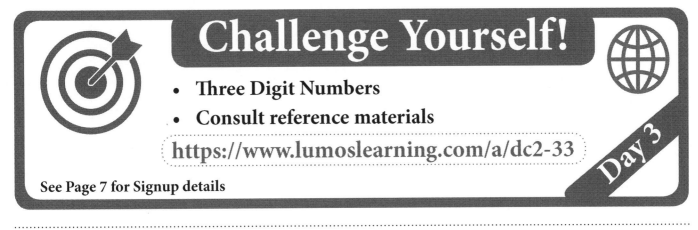

Challenge Yourself!

- Three Digit Numbers
- Consult reference materials

https://www.lumoslearning.com/a/dc2-33

See Page 7 for Signup details

Day 3

Day 4

1. 80 tens equals how many hundreds?

   Ⓐ 80
   Ⓑ 8
   Ⓒ 800
   Ⓓ 88

2. How many groups of hundred can be made from the blocks below?

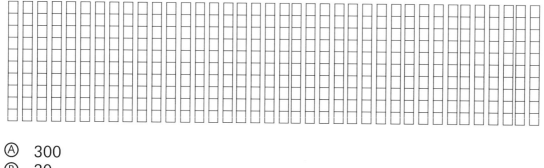

   Ⓐ 300
   Ⓑ 30
   Ⓒ 3
   Ⓓ 380

3. Josh drew 6 hundred base-blocks and 10 ten base-blocks. How many hundreds did Josh's drawing represent?

4. Blake said that 700 ones is more than 70 tens. Is he correct? Explain your answer.

Day 4

Read the story and answer the questions.

It was a nice sunny day outside. Noe and Kevin wanted to ride their bikes to the park. The boys were at Noe's house. They had ridden bikes the day before. Kevin had spent the night with Noe. When they got ready, they noticed their tires were low on air and they needed to fix them.

The boys looked in the garage. Luckily, they found a tire pump. In no time, they had their bikes ready to go!

5. Where were the boys? Mark the answer.

- Ⓐ   At the park
- Ⓑ   At Noe's grandma's house
- Ⓒ   At Kevin's house
- Ⓓ   At Noe's house

6. Who are the characters in the story? Write them.

7. What was the problem in the story? Write your own answer.

8. **If you were to give a speech about making a sandwich which 2 sentences below would be the best ideas to use?**

Ⓐ You could get the materials and make the sandwich while you were talking about it.
Ⓑ You could pass out notes to the class, so they could follow along.
Ⓒ You could eat the sandwich.
Ⓓ You could ask your little brother for help.

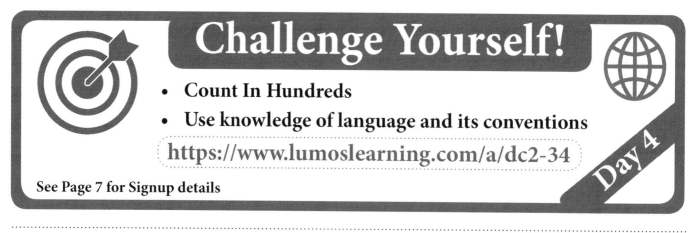

Challenge Yourself!

- **Count In Hundreds**
- **Use knowledge of language and its conventions**

https://www.lumoslearning.com/a/dc2-34

Day 4

See Page 7 for Signup details

Day 5

1. Start at 210 and count by 5's. What is the 6th number you say?

Ⓐ 710
Ⓑ 270
Ⓒ 770
Ⓓ 240

2. Identify the pattern of the numbers by placing a check-mark under the column.

	5s	10s	100s
310, 410, 510, 610, 710, 810			
305, 310, 315, 320, 325, 330			
715, 725, 735, 745, 755, 765			
400, 405, 410, 415, 420, 425			

3. Complete the table by filling in the missing numbers from each pattern.

	545	555		575
803				843
	325	425		
800			830	

4. Ted says that you can start at any number and count by 10s and every number in the pattern will end in a zero. Is Ted correct? Explain your answer.

We speak in different ways when we talk to different people.

Informal speaking is a way we talk to friends and relatives. Formal speaking is a way we talk to people we do not know very well.

5. Read the names in the box and mark if we would talk to them informal or formal.

Word	Informal	Formal
Mother		
Classmate		
Best friend		
Mayor		
President		
Grandma		

6. Read the sentences and write formal or informal after each one.

a. "Hey, let's go swimming!"

b. "Your Honor, would like to invite you to attend our banquet."

c. "This is to inform you of your required attendance."

d. "Let's get this party going!"

e. "Mr. President, we are proud of you.

[   ]

7. Which 2 sentences are informal?

   Ⓐ "Mom, I am hungry!"
   Ⓑ "Enter the building through the door."
   Ⓒ "Pay your bill on time."
   Ⓓ "Yeah, we won the game!"

8. Your teacher told the class to write a letter to the City Council. Which type of English would you use? Formal or Informal?

[   ]

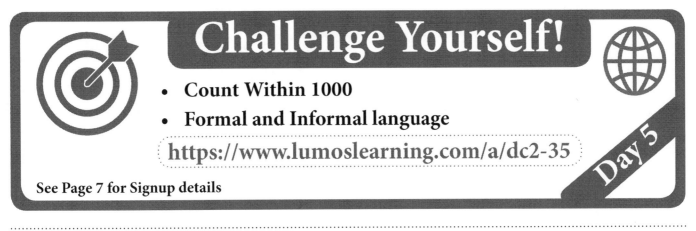

Challenge Yourself!

• Count Within 1000
• Formal and Informal language

https://www.lumoslearning.com/a/dc2-35

Day 5

See Page 7 for Signup details

SUMMER WORD SEARCH

S	A	H	F	L	O	W	E	R	L
T	B	U	T	T	E	R	F	L	Y
A	R	S	E	S	Y	W	I	C	H
W	L	A	L	A	D	Y	B	U	G
B	S	N	A	I	L	L	E	T	R
E	N	E	A	G	O	W	F	R	Y
R	D	R	A	G	O	N	F	L	Y
R	P	I	N	E	A	P	P	L	E
Y	A	I	C	E	C	R	E	A	M
M	U	S	H	R	O	O	M	C	Y

1. Cat 2. Cow 3. Duck 4. Chicken
5. Goat 6. Rooster 7. Turkey 8. Horse
9. Pig 10. Dog 11. Sheep

Answer: COUNTRYSIDE

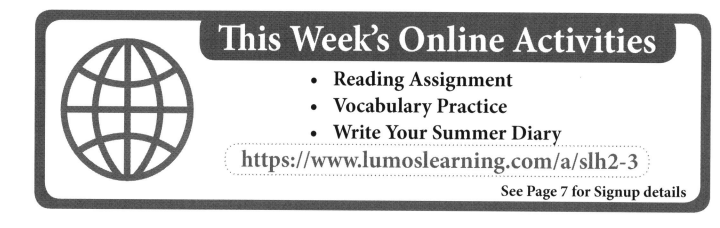

This Week's Online Activities

- **Reading Assignment**
- **Vocabulary Practice**
- **Write Your Summer Diary**

https://www.lumoslearning.com/a/slh2-3

See Page 7 for Signup details

Weekly Fun Summer Photo Contest

📷 Take a picture of your summer fun activity and share it on Twitter or Instagram

\# Use the **#SummerLearning** mention

@LumosLearning on Twitter 🐦 or

@lumos.learning on Instagram 📷

Tag friends and increase your chances of winning the contest

Participate and stand a chance to **WIN $50 Amazon gift card!**

Compare Two Three-digit Numbers (2.NBT.A.4)

Day 1

1. Choose the comparison that is correct.

   Ⓐ   400 + 50 + 2 < 400 + 20 + 5
   Ⓑ   312 > 300 + 20 + 1
   Ⓒ   400 + 60 + 2 = 462
   Ⓓ   900 = 900 + 90

2. Select all of the comparisons that are correct.

   Ⓐ   413 < 400 + 30 + 1
   Ⓑ   500 + 60 + 8 = 568
   Ⓒ   100 + 70 + 7 > 700 + 70 + 1
   Ⓓ   200 + 2 < 200 + 20
   Ⓔ   777 = 700 + 70

3. Which number is the greatest between 324, 342, 234, 243?

4. Place a check mark under the correct column to complete each comparison.

	>	<	=
459 ___ 495			
233 ___ 200 + 30 + 1			
700 + 70 ___ 700 + 7			
200 + 40 ___ 240			

Prefix and Suffix (L.2.4B)

Prefixes are letters added to words to form new words with different meanings. Read the prefix and what it means.

5. Write the definitions of each new word that is made when the prefix is added.
   For example - unlocked - not locked.
   un - not

   a. unhappy - _____

   b. unopened - _____

   c. unable - _____

   d. unknown - _____

6. Read the sentences below. Mark the sentence that has a prefix word in it that means "not".

   Ⓐ He isn't going to the fair because he is sick.
   Ⓑ She untied her shoelaces.
   Ⓒ He is looking for the answer to the question.
   Ⓓ She will reread the book to better understand it.

7. Read the prefix and what it means.

   Write the definitions of each new word that is made when the prefix is added.
   Example: remake – make again re – again, back

   a. reread - _____

   b. replay - _____

   c. redo - _____

8. **The prefix "pre" means before. Read the sentences and highlight the words that have this prefix in it.**

Her little sister went to preschool in the city.

Mom had to preheat the oven before she could cook her supper.

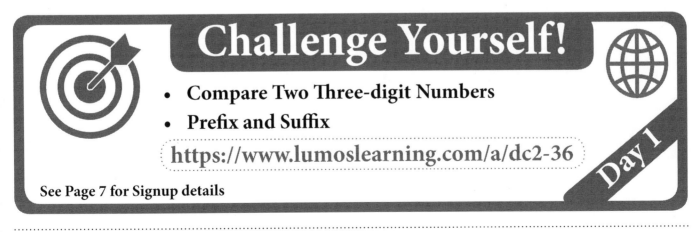

Day 2

1. Select all of the equations that equal 68.

   Ⓐ $78 - 10 = ?$
   Ⓑ $34 + 34 = ?$
   Ⓒ $100 - 28 = ?$
   Ⓓ $22 + 46 = ?$
   Ⓔ $58 + 20 = ?$

2. Select all of the equations that equal 23.

   Ⓐ $53 - 33 = ?$
   Ⓑ $19 + 5 = ?$
   Ⓒ $65 - 42 = ?$
   Ⓓ $3 + 20 = ?$
   Ⓔ $11 + 23 = ?$

3. What number does x represent in the equation?
   $54 + x = 75$

4. Match each equation with the number it equals by placing a checkmark under the correct column.

	27	18	32
$23 + ? = 41$			
$62 - ? = 30$			
$48 - ? = 21$			

Adjectives and Adverbs (L.2.1E)

Adjectives and adverbs are words used in sentences. Adjectives tell about nouns while adverbs tell about verbs, adjectives or another adverb.

5. Read the list of noun phrases. Write the adjectives.

noun phrases	adjectives
purple flowers	
second-grade teacher	
yellow bright light	
funny smile	
grumpy old man	
good grades	

6. Read the sentences and mark the one with 3 adjectives in it.

Ⓐ The pretty little lady was looking for her tiny kitten.
Ⓑ She lost her book and was very sad.
Ⓒ Don't play in the rain today.
Ⓓ We like our cupcakes very much.

7. Choose the correct adjective that will make the sentence correct. Mark your answer.

The _____ pillow helped me sleep.

Ⓐ loudly
Ⓑ first-grade
Ⓒ fluffy
Ⓓ well

8. Choose the correct adjective for each sentence.

Sentence	Adjectives	correct adjective
We are _____ spellers.	well, good	
The _____ spider scared us.	always, huge	
The _____ bike was fun to ride.	very, orange	
My _____ sister let me go with her.	sweet, sweetly	

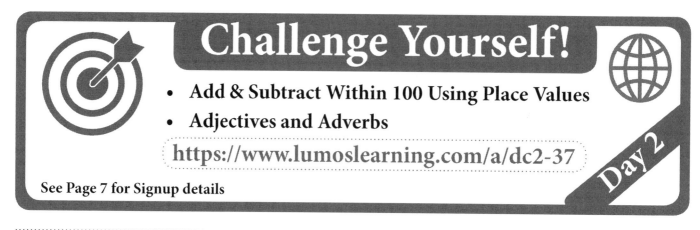

Challenge Yourself!

- Add & Subtract Within 100 Using Place Values
- Adjectives and Adverbs

https://www.lumoslearning.com/a/dc2-37

Day 2

See Page 7 for Signup details

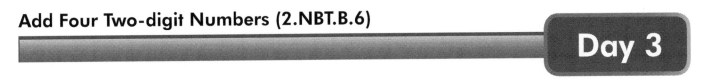
1. Which equation with two addends will give you the same answer as the following equation with four addends?

   $42 + 11 + 14 + 9 = ?$

   Ⓐ $53 + 14 = ?$
   Ⓑ $23 + 11 = ?$
   Ⓒ $42 + 11 = ?$
   Ⓓ $53 + 23 = ?$

2. Which way is NOT another way you can add $21 + 24 + 55 + 2 = ?$

   Ⓐ $(21 + 24) + (55 + 2) = ?$
   Ⓑ $(21 + 2) + (55 + 24) = ?$
   Ⓒ $(2 + 24) + (55 + 21) = ?$
   Ⓓ $(21 + 55) + (21 + 2) = ?$

3. What is the sum of $43 + 54 + 20 + 5$?

4. Match each equation with its correct sum by placing a check mark under the correct column for each equation. Some columns might have more than one check, some columns might not have a check.

	110	121	111
28 + 17 + 44 + 22			
39 + 18 + 24 + 29			
6 + 68 + 12 + 25			

Day 3

Context clues can be words or phrases in sentences that help you to understand what the meaning of the sentence is when you are reading.

Context clues are useful in understanding words that are spelled the same, sound the same, but have different meanings.

5. **Read the sentences below. Highlight the words that are spelled and sound the same but have different meanings In each pair of sentences.**

He broke his big toe.

She spent her money and was broke now.

The iron nail was rusty.

Mom will iron Dad's shirt.

The cave was dark.

The rain made the roof cave in.

6. **Read the words and sentences. Choose the word that will make sense. Be careful as some words sound the same but are spelled differently and mean different things. Other words are spelled the same but have different meanings when used. Write the words in the blanks that belong. A word can be used more than one time.**

mind
flower
flour
handle
stare

1. The handle of the milk jug was slippery.	
2. I always mind my parents.	
3. She did not stare at the strange looking car.	
4. What kind of flower is your favorite?	
5. What's on your mind?	
6. You need to use flour when you make a cake.	

7. Some words are rhyming words. Read the words and match them to their rhyming words in the box.

sing _____
fox _____
believe _____
scout _____

Ⓐ about
Ⓑ relieve
Ⓒ ring
Ⓓ box

8. Read the words below. Highlight the two words in each row that sound the same but mean something different.

pies piece peace
knows nose knew

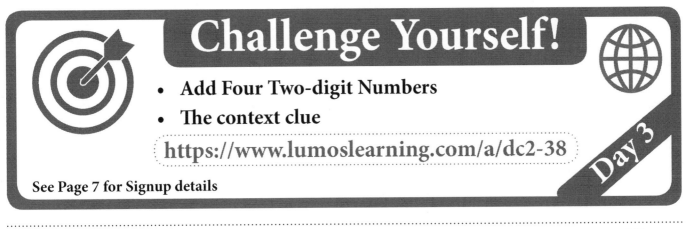

Challenge Yourself!

• Add Four Two-digit Numbers
• The context clue

https://www.lumoslearning.com/a/dc2-38

Day 3

See Page 7 for Signup details

Day 4

1. What is the value of x in the equation 109 + x = 309?

   Ⓐ 481
   Ⓑ 200
   Ⓒ 208
   Ⓓ 408

2. What is the value of x in the equation 385 – x = 300.

   Ⓐ 685
   Ⓑ 680
   Ⓒ 0
   Ⓓ 85

3. What is the difference between 825 and 399?

4. Match each equation with its correct sum or difference by placing a check mark under the correct column for each equation. Some columns might have more than one check, some columns might not have a check.

	313	303	302	312
124 + 179				
572 - 259				
491 - 189				
209 + 103				

Day 4

Root words are main words. If letters are added to a root word, it becomes a new word. An example: help + ful = helpful.

5. Read the sentences and decide which is the best definition of the underlined word. The students need <u>additional</u> time to finish their work.

Ⓐ less
Ⓑ excellent
Ⓒ larger
Ⓓ more

5.1 We were <u>thankful</u> that our cat was not hurt.

Ⓐ full of thanks
Ⓑ not happy
Ⓒ full of regret
Ⓓ very sad

5.2 It was <u>thoughtful</u> of her to help the elderly lady.

Ⓐ rude
Ⓑ kind
Ⓒ useless
Ⓓ not important

6. Make new words by adding the ending to the root word. Write your answers.

care + ful =	
hope + less =	
break + able =	
thank + ful =	

7. **Read the words and decide which endings were added to make the new words. Write the ending next to each word.**

comfortable = _____

hopeless = _____

respectful = _____

playful = _____

8. **Read the words in the box and write the correct root word for each of them.**

Word	Word	Word	Root word
respectful	respected	respects	
careless	careful	caring	
playful	played	playing	
breakable	breaking	breaks	

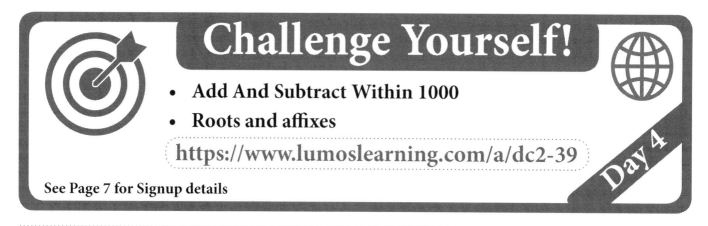

Day 5

1. Which statement is true?

Ⓐ   399 is 10 more than 299.
Ⓑ   418 is 10 less than 408.
Ⓒ   977 is 100 more than 877.
Ⓓ   208 is 10 more than 218.

2. Select all of the true statements below.

Ⓐ   877 is 10 less than 887.
Ⓑ   480 is 100 less than 380.
Ⓒ   763 is 10 more than 663.
Ⓓ   111 is 100 less than 211.
Ⓔ   689 is 10 more than 699.

3. What number is 10 more than 999?

4. Place a check mark under each column that make the statements true.

	10 more	10 less	100 more	100 less
546 is ____ than 536			.	
297 is ____ than 397				
891 is ____ than 901				
1000 is ____ than 900				

Connecting related words (L.2.4D)

Compound words are made by joining two words to make a new word.

5. Read the words and write the compound words next to them.

ham + burger =	
pop + corn =	
milk + shake =	
butter + fly =	
tooth + brush =	

6. Read the list of words and make new compound words from other words in the list. Write them in ABC order.

ball
bell
home
end
foot
work
week
door

7. Read the sentences and highlight the compound word in each sentence.

A. Chloe loves to go horseback riding.

B. Sam got a new skateboard!

C. What is wrong with Grandma?

D. Someone found my lost dog.

E. Watermelon is my favorite dessert.

8. Which compound word would be used if I am talking about something I carry my books in? Mark your answer.

Ⓐ firewood
Ⓑ snowman
Ⓒ backpack
Ⓓ cupcake

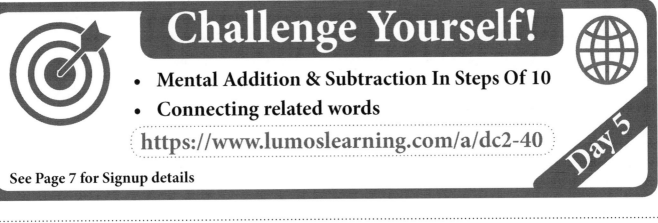

Challenge Yourself!

• Mental Addition & Subtraction In Steps Of 10
• Connecting related words

https://www.lumoslearning.com/a/dc2-40

Day 5

See Page 7 for Signup details

This Week's Online Activities

- Reading Assignment
- Vocabulary Practice
- Write Your Summer Diary

https://www.lumoslearning.com/a/slh2-3

See Page 7 for Signup details

Weekly Fun Summer Photo Contest

Take a picture of your summer fun activity and share it on Twitter or Instagram

Use the **#SummerLearning** mention

@LumosLearning on Twitter or

@lumos.learning on Instagram

Tag friends and increase your chances of winning the contest

Participate and stand a chance to WIN $50 Amazon gift card!

Bundle Of Tens (2.NBT.A.1.A)

Day 1

1. Which choice represents 213?

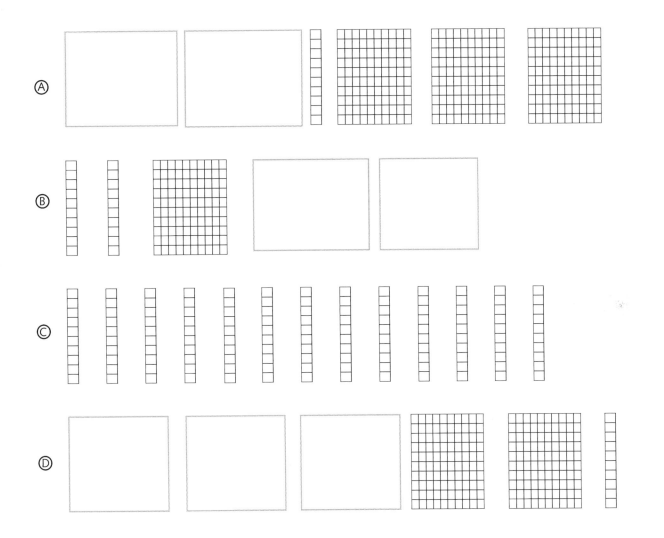

2. Choose the choice that the blocks below represent.

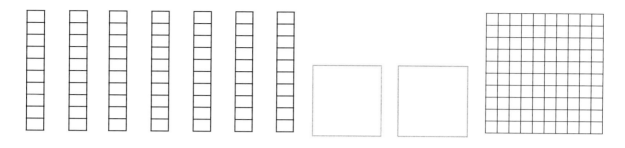

   Ⓐ 7 hundreds, 1 ten, 2 ones
   Ⓑ 7 tens , 2 hundreds, 1 one
   Ⓒ 1 hundred, 2 ones, 7 tens
   Ⓓ 2 hundreds, 7 tens, 2 ones

3. What number is represented by the blocks?

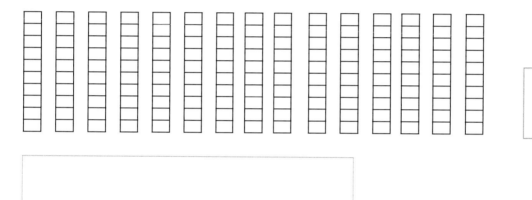

4. Place a check under the correct column to tell whether the number is less than 300 or more than 300.

	Less than 300	More than 300
13 tens, 200 ones		
14 tens, 150 ones		
27 tens, 3 ones		
15 ones, 20 tens		

Words can be related to each other in their meaning. Some words can be weaker or stronger than others. Example: big, gigantic would be in order from weaker to stronger.

5. Read the words below. Put them in the box in order from weaker to stronger meaning.

frightened
afraid

Weaker	Stronger

6. Choose the words that describe more than the underlined words in the sentences. Write them in the blanks.

frightened
awful
gorgeous
gigantic

a. Their dresses were <u>very pretty.</u>

b. Madeline was <u>very scared</u> when she saw the lion.

c. The spoiled milk tasted <u>very bad.</u>

d. The elephant was <u>very big.</u>

7. Read the words and sentences below. Write the correct antonym for the underlined words.

closed
yes
play
there

1. She said no to her mother.	
2. They wanted to work.	
3. The door was open.	
4. We were here when it started to rain.	

8. Some words that help us to read and write are opposites of other words. They are called antonyms. Read the words below and match them to their antonyms.

short	**tall**
happy	
left	
fast	
on	
hot	

(cold, sad, slow, right, off)

Challenge Yourself!

- Bundle Of Tens
- The meaning of words

https://www.lumoslearning.com/a/dc2-41

Day 1

See Page 7 for Signup details

1. Lucy drew a line that was 7 inches. Select all of the possible representations of Lucy's line.

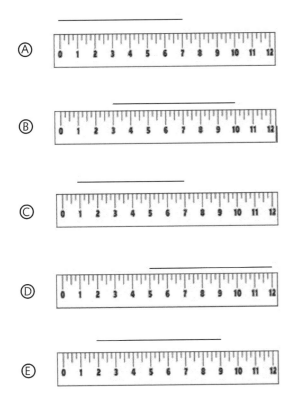

2. Travis cut a piece of ribbon that was 9 cm long. Which one of the following choices could be where Travis placed the ribbon on the ruler?

   Ⓐ Travis' ribbon began on 3 cm and ended on 9 cm
   Ⓑ Travis' ribbon began on 1 cm and ended on 9 cm
   Ⓒ Travis' ribbon ended on 14 cm and began on 5 cm
   Ⓓ Travis' ribbon ended on 19 cm and began on 27 cm

3. Kaylie placed her pencil on the ruler starting at 3 cm. If her pencil is 14 cm long, what number did Kaylie's pencil end on?

4. Match each line on the ruler with its length in inches.

	7 inches	2 inches	5 inches	9 inches
(ruler 1)				
(ruler 2)				
(ruler 3)				
(ruler 4)				

Day 2

5. We use or think of words that tell about real-life things that we know or happen to us.

Read the words, then match them to the clue words in the box.

	bright, colorful half-circle in the sky, pot of gold	baby dog, cute 4-legged pet	desktop, laptop, technology tool	buddy, pal, companion
friend				
computer				
puppy				
rainbow				

6. **Read the words and sentences below. Choose the word that would best fit in the blank, given the real-life clues after each sentence. Use each word only one time.**

   (shout, recess, laugh, playground)

   a. Most of the kids go to the _____ on Saturday to have fun. CLUE: slide, swing, equipment

   b. He would _____ so loud at the jokes, his face would turn red. CLUE: chuckle, giggle

   c. Jeff's favorite thing at school is _____. CLUE: friends, play, outside, games

   d. My ears hurt every time I hear her _____! CLUE: scream, yell, holler

7. **Some words fall into categories (real-life groups) of things we know well.**
   Read the words and mark the best categories. Mark only 1 category for each word.

	Farm Animals	Indoor Pet Animals	Wild or Jungle Animals
cow			
dog			
horse			
elephant			
chicken			
lion			
hamster			
giraffe			
bear			

8. **Read the words below and choose the ones that describe a stuffed animal. Mark your answer.**

   Ⓐ hard, prickly, rough
   Ⓑ soft, cuddly, huggable

Challenge Yourself!

- **Measuring Length Of Objects**
- **Usage of words**

  https://www.lumoslearning.com/a/dc2-42

  Day 2

See Page 7 for Signup details

Day 3

1. **Look at the line on the ruler below. Choose the statement that correctly describes the measurement.**

Ⓐ The line is 8 inches long.
Ⓑ The line is 8 centimeters long.
Ⓒ The line is 3 inches long.
Ⓓ The line is 3 ½ inches long.

2. **Look at the line on the ruler below. Choose the true statement.**

Ⓐ The line is about 3 inches.
Ⓑ The line is about 3 centimeters.
Ⓒ The line is close to 8 inches.
Ⓓ The line is shorter than 4 centimeters.

3. **Kylie had a pencil that was 10 centimeters. She sharpened it and now it is 8 centimeters. How many centimeters were taken off when Kylie sharpened her pencil?**

4. **Look at the ruler below. Then match each statement as true or false by placing a check-mark under each column.**

	True	False
9 centimeters is shorter than $^3/_{12}$ inches		
4 ½ inches is between 11 and 12 centimeters		
5 inches is closer to 13 centimeters than 12 centimeters		

Day 3

5. Verbs describe actions. The list below has verbs in it that are similar (related) to each other.

Choose the verbs that would describe what you could do with a ball. Mark your answer.

- (A) eat, drink, smack, drool, sip, slurp
- (B) toss, drop, throw, hurl, pitch, bounce

6. Read the list of related verbs and match them to another verb that is like them in the box.

chat, talk	
tired, drowsy	
weep, sob	
tidy, clean	

(neat, cry, sleepy, speak)

7. Read the sentence below. Find the adjective that is related to good and write it.

The boys did an excellent job on their project.

```

```

8. Read the sentences below. Mark the one that uses a verb related to laugh.

- (A) They cried when the puppy was hurt.
- (B) She giggled when she saw the funny face on the clown.
- (C) He wanted to slurp his drink.
- (D) The teacher was happy with the good work her class did

Challenge Yourself!

- Measure Length Of Object Using Two Different Length Units
- Shades of word meaning

https://www.lumoslearning.com/a/dc2-43

Day 3

See Page 7 for Signup details

Day 4

1. The length of a sheet of paper is about 18 _____?

   Ⓐ Centimeters
   Ⓑ Feet
   Ⓒ Inches
   Ⓓ Meters

2. The height of a refrigerator is about 2 ___?

   Ⓐ Centimeters
   Ⓑ Feet
   Ⓒ Inches
   Ⓓ Meters

3. Angelica <u>correctly</u> answered the question "About how many inches is a ruler?" What number did Angelica say?

4. Complete the table by filling in the unit that is the best estimate for each row.

	Centimeter	Feet	Inches	Meters
The height of a birthday candle is about 2 __?				
The height of a chair is about 1 __?				
The height of a box of cereal is about 12 __?				
The height of a vacuum cleaner is about 4 __?				

Day 4

Read the conversation below. Answer the questions about the words. Remember that adjectives describe nouns, verbs tell action, and adverbs help the verb.

George <u>said</u>, "Let's go on a hike in the <u>deep</u> woods today!"

"No way!" <u>shouted</u> Timothy. "I am <u>frightened</u> of the <u>dark</u> woods."

"Don't be <u>scared</u>!" George <u>replied</u>. "We'll take my <u>guard</u> dog with us. Smokey is a <u>great watch</u> dog. He will keep us safe from <u>harm</u>."

1. Which words describe the woods? Write them.

2. Which words tell about being afraid? Write them.

3. Which words below tell how George and Timothy talked? Mark 3 words from the story.

- Ⓐ answered
- Ⓑ spoke
- Ⓒ replied
- Ⓓ said
- Ⓔ shouted

4. **Use the words below and write a conversation between you and a friend. Be sure to use quotation marks, capital letters, and punctuation correctly.**

bright sunlight

wonderful playground

joyfully swinging

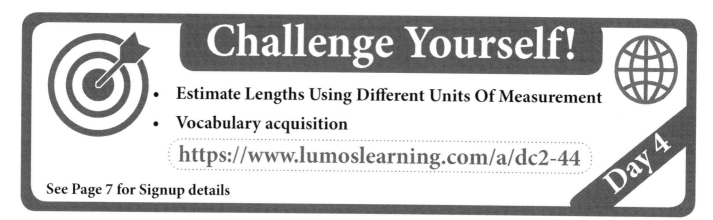

Challenge Yourself!

- Estimate Lengths Using Different Units Of Measurement
- Vocabulary acquisition

https://www.lumoslearning.com/a/dc2-44

Day 4

See Page 7 for Signup details

1. Choose the correct comparison about Rectangle A and B below

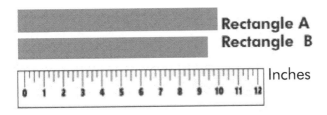

Rectangle A
Rectangle B

Inches

Ⓐ   Rectangle A is 1 inch longer than Rectangle B.
Ⓑ   Rectangle A is ½ centimeter longer than Rectangle B.
Ⓒ   Rectangle B is ½ inch shorter than Rectangle A.
Ⓓ   Rectangle B is 1 inch shorter than Rectangle B.

2. Choose the correct comparison about Rectangle A and B below.

Rectangle A
Rectangle B

cm   1   2   3   4   5   6   7   8   9   10   11   12   13   14
inches   1   2   3   4   5

Ⓐ   Rectangle B is 4 inches longer than Rectangle A.
Ⓑ   Rectangle A is 4 cm shorter than Rectangle B.
Ⓒ   Rectangle A is 8 cm shorter than Rectangle B.
Ⓓ   Rectangle B is 12 inches longer than Rectangle A.

3. How many inches longer is Rectangle A than Rectangle B.

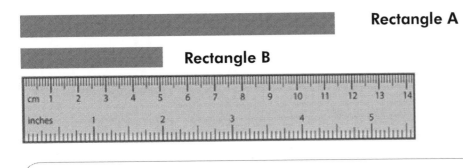

Rectangle A

Rectangle B

cm   1   2   3   4   5   6   7   8   9   10   11   12   13   14
inches   1   2   3   4   5

4. Bubble in the circle under the correct statement for each row.

	Line A is 6 cm shorter than Line B.	Line A and Line B are the same length.	Line A is 1 inch longer than Line B.	Line B is 4 inches shorter than Line A.
Line A / Line B with cm ruler (0–12)	○	○	○	○
Line A / Line B with cm and inches ruler (0–14)	○	○	○	○
Line A / Line B with ruler (0–11)	○	○	○	○
Line A / Line B with cm and inches ruler (0–14)	○	○	○	○

Day 5

Informative/Explanatory Writing

You read information about many things. When we write or read passages that tell or inform us, we call it informative, or explanatory writing. Your science and social studies books have this kind of writing.

Informative writing includes a topic sentence that tells what you are about to read.

Then important facts are given to tell you more. These facts give examples to support them.

At the end of the writing, there is a concluding statement that retells the topic sentence.

5. What does an informative/explanatory piece of writing tell you? Mark the best answer.

Ⓐ It gives you examples.
Ⓑ It has a topic sentence.
Ⓒ It has a conclusion.
Ⓓ It tells or informs you about things.

Read the information below and answer the question no 2, 3 & 4

Spring

We see weather changes along with new animal and plant life in the Spring.
Spring is a season that comes after winter and before summer. The weather is not as cold as in winter. The sun rises earlier in the morning and sets later in the afternoon during Spring. The months when Spring occurs in the U.S. are March through May.
Flowers bloom in Spring and trees have new leaves. Many people grow flowers and vegetables during this season.
Animals also have babies during Spring. Birds and rabbits can be seen more outside.

6. Which is the topic sentence in the writing?

Ⓐ The months when Spring occurs in the U.S. are March through May.
Ⓑ We see weather changes along with new animal and plant life in the Spring.
Ⓒ Many people grow flowers and vegetables during this season.
Ⓓ Flowers bloom in Spring and trees have new leaves.

7. What are the 3 facts that are used in the writing about Spring?

Ⓐ Animals have babies
Ⓑ School is out
Ⓒ Dogs bark
Ⓓ Flowers bloom and leaves grow
Ⓔ Weather is cooler

8. The writing does not have a concluding statement. Choose the sentence that would best help to end this writing about Spring.

Ⓐ Spring has weather changes.
Ⓑ Leaves come out.
Ⓒ Baby birds are born
Ⓓ Spring brings cooler weather and new life for animals and plants.

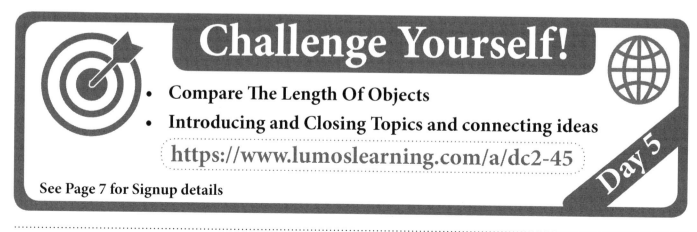

Challenge Yourself!

- Compare The Length Of Objects
- Introducing and Closing Topics and connecting ideas

https://www.lumoslearning.com/a/dc2-45

Day 5

See Page 7 for Signup details

This Week's Online Activities

- **Reading Assignment**
- **Vocabulary Practice**
- **Write Your Summer Diary**

https://www.lumoslearning.com/a/slh2-3

See Page 7 for Signup details

Weekly Fun Summer Photo Contest

📷 Take a picture of your summer fun activity and share it on Twitter or Instagram

Use the **#SummerLearning** mention

@LumosLearning on Twitter or

@lumos.learning on Instagram

↗ Tag friends and increase your chances of winning the contest

Participate and stand a chance to WIN $50 Amazon gift card!

Week 10

Lumos Short Story Competition 2022

Write a short story based on your summer experiences and get a chance to win $100 cash prize + 1 year free subscription to Lumos StepUp + trophy with a certificate.
To enter the competition follow the instructions.

Step 1

Visit **www.lumoslearning.com/a/tg2-3**
and register for online fun summer program.

Step 2

After registration, your child can upload their summer story by logging into the student portal and clicking on **Lumos Short Story Competition 2022.**

Note: *If you have already registered this book and using online resources need not register again. Students can simply log in to the student portal and submit their story for the competition.*
Visit: www.lumoslearning.com/a/slh2022 for more information

Last date for submission is August 31, 2022

Use the space provided below for scratch work before uploading your summer story Scratch Work

2021 Winning Story

In March 2020, I found out that my 7th-grade exams were canceled. At first, I was excited, but I soon realized that these changes would upend my expectations for school. Over time, my classmates and I realized that the global coronavirus pandemic was not something to be excited about and would have long-lasting effects on our education. My school canceled exams again this year, and, strangely, I found myself missing them. The virus has revealed global inequality regarding health.

Even as America fights the virus, so is it also fighting racism and injustice. The Black Lives Matter movement has shown me how brutal racism can be. The deaths of George Floyd and Breonna Taylor, two African Americans killed by police for no reason, have made me aware of the dangerous injustice in America. Hatred and violence against Asian immigrants are also on the rise. People of color in the US are routinely subjected to prejudice, if not also violence, at the hands of white people. Chinese people are blamed for the "China virus,"; which has led to Asian Americans being attacked. Enduring forms of racism are preventing progress around the world. Racism in society takes many forms, including prejudice, discrimination, and microaggressions. If racism is systemic in America, there will never be true peace or equality until it is uprooted. People see me as a person of color and assume that I'm from Africa because of the color of my skin, even though I am half Black and half white. I don't seem to earn as much respect as a white person would because I am thought of as a foreigner, not a true American. It makes me feel unwelcome and unwanted. I am lucky to have access to technology to keep me engaged in learning. There are still others who don't have the ability to continue learning, whose educational institutions have been shut down by the virus. I have learned that so many people lack access to basic necessities and that racism in America continues to lead to violence and injustice. I aspire to work toward a system that addresses these inequalities in the future. This summer I reflected back on all these things and have learned that no matter what, we all should continue to push on, even through hardships and obstacles.

Submit Your Story Online & WIN Prizes!!!

Student Name: Lillian Olson
Grade: 4

2020 Winning Story

Finding Fun during a Pandemic

This was a weird summer. We did not travel because of COVID-19 and stayed mostly at home and outside around our house. Even when I saw my friends, it was unusual. This summer, I worked and made money helping my parents.

The pandemic allowed me to spend more time inside and I learned many new skills. We made face masks and had to figure out which pattern fits us the best. My sister and I enjoyed creating other arts and crafts projects. Additionally, I have been learning to play instruments such as the piano, guitar, and trombone. We also baked and cooked because we did not go out to eat (at all!). I love baking desserts. The brownies and cookies we made were amazing! I also read for one hour a day and did a workbook by Lumos Learning. I especially loved Math.

Our time outdoors was different this summer. We ordered hens. My family spent a lot of time fixing the coop and setting it up for our 18 chickens. We had a daily responsibility to take care of our chickens in the morning, giving them food and water and in the evening, securing them in their coop. We were surprised that 3 of the hens were actually roosters! Additionally, we exhausted many days gardening and building a retaining wall. Our garden has many different fruits and vegetables. The retaining wall required many heavy bricks, shoveling rocks, and moving dirt around. To cool off from doing all this hard work, we jumped in a stream and went tubing. Our dog, Coco liked to join us.

COVID-19 has also caused me to interact differently with my friends. We used FaceTime, Zoom, and Messenger Kids to chat and video talk with each other. Video chatting is not as fun as being in person with my friends. I love Messenger Kids because it is fun and you can play interactive games with each other.

I had to spend some of my time working. I helped clean my parents' Airbnb. This was busier because of COVID-19. My sister and I will start to sell the chicken eggs once they start to lay which we expect to happen anytime. We had a small business two years ago doing this same thing.

Summer 2020 has been unusual in many ways. We played indoors and outdoors at our house and nearby with family. I have learned new skills and learned to use technology in different ways. Summer of 2020 will never be forgotten!

Submit Your Story Online & WIN Prizes!!!

Answer Key &
Detailed Explanations

Question No.	Answer	Detailed Explanation
1	D	The answer is D. 71 pages are the total and a part to subtract is 23 pages. 71 minus 23 is 48
2	A	The answer is A. If Kim has 24 pieces after she gave 17 away, then you must add the numbers to find out how much she had before giving any away. 24 plus 17 equals 41.
3	B	The answer is B. Lucy had 14 and her father gave her 26, so you should add those numbers together. 14 plus 26 equals 40. She went and bought an art kit for 15 dollars, so you should subtract to show that money being taken away. 40 minus 15 equals 25.
4	D	The answer is D. There are 43 grapes in the bag, in order to find out how many were in there at first you have to add what was taken out. 43 plus 11 (Brad) plus 14 (Jay) equals 68.
5	D	The best answer is D. It includes all of those that went to the beach. Answer A and B only include some of those and is not correct. Answer C cannot be found in the story and is incorrect.
6	C	They had been in the water before and Dad said they could go back in. The water is correct. The table, the van and none of the above are not correct, as they are not in the story details
7	B, C, D, G	Dog leash, shells, and purse were not listed as things that Sara took to the beach. They are not correct. Sunscreen, sand shovel and tools and bathing suit are listed and are correct.
8	-	Sample Answer: They went home because it was getting dark. At the end of the story it is noted that it was getting dark. That would be the reason they went home. The student must say that in his/her sentence, but word choice can vary.

Question No.	Answer	Detailed Explanation
1	A & C	The answers are A and C, because they both equal 16 when added together.
2	B & D	The answers are B & D, because they both equal 7 when subtracted.
3	B & C	The answers are B & C. The difference of 14 minus 2 is 12. The sum of 9 plus 3 is 12.
4	A,B,C&E	The answers are A, B, C, and E, because they all equal 20 when the addends are added together.
5	-	The story begins with the princess and her name, so sentence #2 should be first. Then the story states how the princess and bird sang at night. The clue for the sentence to be second is "in the beginning". The bird then told her how to get her hair back to red when the witch cast the spell. It should go third. The last sentence should be they got married and lived happily ever after, as that is the ending of the story.
6	D	The main idea is that good wins over evil. The fourth answer is the only correct one that is the main idea of the folktale. The first answer is not given. The second answer is not supported, and neither is the third.
7	A	All of the sentences are details in the story, but sentence A is the correct one. It tells exactly what the prince did. The story goes on to say that because of that a rose bush grew.
8	B,C	The first and fourth sentences are details from the story. They are correct. The second and third sentences are not in the story.

Question No.	Answer	Detailed Explanation
1	A	The answer is A. Even numbers are numbers that are divisible by 2. Even numbers have 0,2,4,6,8 in the ones place.
2	C	The answer is C. 6 plus 6 equals 12 and 12 is an even number. Two even numbers will always equal an even number. Two odd numbers will always equal an even number. An even and an odd number will always equal an odd number.
3	D	The answer is D. 3 plus 6 equals 9 and 9 is an odd number. An even and an odd number will always equal an odd number. Two even numbers will always equal an even number. Two odd numbers will always equal an odd number.
4	C	The answer choice C is correct. 22, 48, and 30 are all even numbers and 17 is the only odd number in the choices given. Hence, 17 could be the number of socks that James has.
5	C	The story states that the boys wanted to learn how to fly a kite. The third answer is correct. The other answers are not found in the story.
6	B, C	The story states that the boys first did not know what kind of kite to get and then did not know where to fly their kite. The second and third answers are correct. The first and fourth answers are not found in the story and are not correct.
7	B	Some of the boys wanted a dragon kite. Others wanted one with a long tail. They decided to buy one that had a long tail and was a dragon. The second sentence is correct and found in the story. The other sentences are not found in the story and are not correct.
8	A	The first paragraph is the best answer as it is the solution found in the story. The second choice has nothing to do with the second problem.

Day 4

Question No.	Answer	Detailed Explanation
1	C	The answer is C. There are 3 rows and 5 circles in each row. You should add 5 three times.
2	A	The answer is A. There are 5 rows and 4 circles in each row. You should add 4 five times.
3	B	The answer is B. There are 6 rows and 2 circles in each row. You should add 2 six times.
4	A	The answer is A. $4 + 4 + 4 = 12$.
5	A	The first sentence is the best answer, as the rhyming words help the story to flow and give details to help the reader picture the event happening. The second, third and fourth answers are incorrect as they do not back up the poem or its meaning.
6	D	In each verse (except the last line), the first and fourth lines rhyme and the second and third lines rhyme. The last answer is correct.
7	-	The words that rhyme with clown in the poem are down, town, brown and are the only correct answers.
8	C	Alliteration means a way of adding more interest by using words with the same consonant sound at the beginning of them. The third sentence does this with dipping dark deep down. It is the correct answer.

Question No.	Answer	Detailed Explanation
1	C	The answer is C because there are 4 hundreds, 2 tens, and 3 ones.
2	A	The answer is A. 3 hundreds, 2 tens, and 7 ones is 327.
3	D	The answer is D. 5 hundreds, 6 tens, and 8 ones is 568.
4	B	The answer is B. 58 has 5 tens and 8 ones, but it does not have hundreds.
5	A	The first answer is the best answer because it states the setting and tells you what Chloe does to help out and what she finds. The second and third animals are details but do not explain. The fourth answer does not follow the story line.
6	C,B,A,D	First stated in the story is that Chloe is at her Nana and Grandpa's house. Then the story goes on to say she helps feed and water the horses. Next, she hears a baby chick and last Grandpa picks up the chick. This is the correct story sequence.
7	-	Answers will vary but should include that the story setting shows where Chloe is when the story happens and helps you to understand what happens all the way to the end.
8	C	The third sentence is the only one that is NOT found in the story and is the correct answer

Day 1

Question No.	Answer	Detailed Explanation
1	A	The answer is A. There are 10 tens in a hundred. If there are 5 hundreds then it is $10 + 10 + 10 + 10 + 10 = 50$.
2	B	The answer is B. Each block represents a hundred. There are 3 hundred blocks so there are 3 groups of 100
3	C	The answer is C. There are 100 ones in a hundred. If there are 2 hundred blocks then $100 + 100 = 200$ ones.
4	A	The answer is A. There are 4 hundreds blocks. So 400 is represented.
5	D	The fourth sentence is a detail that was used to show Melony that Tabitha was hurt. It is the correct answer. The other quotes do not show that and are not correct.
6	-	Answer will vary but should include that the girls say that they love her, she is the best or similar answers to that.
7	A, C	The story narrative shows that Ms. Sally was kind and caring. It also shows that she was worried. The first and third sentences are correct. The second and fourth sentences are not shown in the narrative of the story and are not correct.
8	A	The sentence is written in capital letters and with explanation marks. This shows that it should be read very loud and with excitement. The first sentence is the only correct one.

Day 2

Question No.	Answer	Detailed Explanation
1	D	The answer is D. The pattern is counting by 5s and the next number is 255.
2	A	The answer is A. The pattern is counting by 100s, so the missing number is 300.
3	D	The answer is D. If you start at 67 and count by tens from 67 you say 77, 87, 97, 107. 107 is the 4th number.
4	A, D& E	The answers are A, D, & E.
5	-	1. Mimi 2. Adelle Characters are the people in the story. Mimi and Adelle are the only characters in this story.
6	-	1. Finland 2. Denmark 3. Mississippi 4. Texas 5. Elvis 6. Denmark 7. Arkansas 8. Pennsylvania 9. Oklahoma 10. Finland Using the story and picture, you can put the spoons in the order they appear.
7	-	Answer will vary but should state something to the effect that they love each other and have a good relationship.
8	C	The third answer is correct. It states that the setting is at Mimi's house in Georgia.

Question No.	Answer	Detailed Explanation
1	C	The answer is C. When writing a number in expanded form you add the value of each number. A 4 in the hundreds place has a value of 400. A 5 in the tens place has a value of 50. A 8 in the ones place has a value of 8.
2	B	The answer is B. 530.
3	C	The answer is C. When writing a number in expanded form you add the value of each number. A 2 in the hundreds place has a value of 200. A 8 in the ones place has a value of 8.
4	A	The answer is A. When writing a number, you write the number how you say it. It is important that students remember to not say "and" when saying whole numbers.
5	C	The fairy tale states that the porridge was hot. It is stated that is why they went for a walk. The third sentence is correct. The other answers are not found and are not correct.
6	-	Answers will vary. The correct answer should say the she was hungry, as that is a detail in the story.
7	C	The story states that she was found asleep in a bed. The third answer is correct. The other answers are not found and are not correct.
8	A	The first sentence describes Goldilocks and is correct. The other sentences give details, but do not tell about her and are not correct.

Day 4

Question No.	Answer	Detailed Explanation
1	B	The answer is B. When comparing numbers, you can begin in the highest places and compare the digits in that place. If the digits are the same, you can move to the next lower place. The 4s in the hundreds place are the same, so you move to the tens place. 8 is greater than 5, so 485 is greater than 458.
2	A	The answer is A. When comparing numbers, you can begin in the highest places and compare the digits in that place. If the digits are the same, you can move to the next lower place. The 2s in the hundreds place are the same, so you move to the tens place. 7 is greater than 6, so 276 is greater than 267.
3	B	The answer is B. When comparing numbers, you can begin in the highest places and compare the digits in that place. If the digits are the same, you can move to the next lower place. The 4s in the hundreds place are the same, so you move to the tens place. 8 is greater than 0, so 480 is greater than 408.
4	D	The answer is D. When comparing numbers, you can begin in the highest places and compare the digits in that place. If the digits are the same, you can move to the next lower place.
5	C	The third answer is the best answer as it is found in the passage. The other answers are not complete and are not correct.
6	-	The passage states that they are made by people at their houses, do not come from a store and are not made in a factory. So, the answers are **houses**, **store**, and **factory**.
7	-	Answers will vary but should include that it is too heavy to move without a trailer and/or that it is put on a trailer to move it around.
8	B	The best answer is the second sentence. It tells the main idea of the passage. It is the correct answer. The first, third, and fourth sentences are not found in the passage.

Question No.	Answer	Detailed Explanation
1	B	The answer is B. When finding a missing addend, you can subtract the other addend from the whole. 44 minus 12 equals 32.
2	D	The answer is D. To find a missing minuend in a subtraction problem, you add the subtrahend to the difference.
3	B	The answer is 34. When finding a missing addend, you can subtract the other addend from the whole. 55 minus 21 equals 34.
4	D	The answer is D. 100 minus 25 equals 75. It does NOT equal 76.
5	D	The main topic of the article is to give facts about the rainforest. The fourth sentence is correct, the other sentences are details and are not correct.
6	-	The sentence is the main topic sentence of the article. The missing words to be filled in should be "Tropical rainforests". That is the only correct answer.
7	-	1. hibiscus 2. orchard 3. passion flower
8	-	The articles gives examples of snakes both on land and in the water. So that column should be marked for snakes. The others should be marked for land only as the article does not state that these could live in the water.

Question No.	Answer	Detailed Explanation
1	B	The answer is B. You can set the problem up vertically to add them altogether, or you can break it apart and add two numbers at a time. $10 + 45 = 55$ $55 + 10 = 65$ $65 + 20 = 85$.
2	A	The answer is A. You can set the problem up vertically to add them altogether, or you can break it apart and add two numbers at a time. $15 + 15 = 30$ $30 + 20 = 50$ $50 + 30 = 80$.
3	D	The answer is 46. You can set the problem up vertically to add them altogether, or you can break it apart and add two numbers at a time. $12 + 10 = 22$ $22 + 16 = 38$ $38 + 8 = 46$.
4	C	The answer is C. You can set the problem up vertically to add them altogether, or you can break it apart and add two numbers at a time.
5	B,D	The second and fourth sentences show how the events of his life are connected and how he helped our country. They are correct. The second and third sentences are details but do not show how he helped. They are not correct.
6	-	England ruled at that time. It is stated in the second paragraph and is the only correct answer
7	B,C,D,A	The events that show a connection to history are that George joined the war against England, became a general, President of the United States and was important to our country. This is the correct order for the question.
8	A	The first sentence is a detail in the life of George Washington but does not help you to see how he helped our country. It is the correct answer. The other answers show how he helped and are not correct.

Day 2

Question No.	Answer	Detailed Explanation
1	D	The answer is D. 763 minus 211 equals 552.
2	A	The answer is A. 287 plus 109 equals 396.
3	C	The answer is C. Sums are answers to addition problems. 418 plus 220 equals 638.
4	A	The answer is A. Differences are answers to subtraction problems. 733 minus 190 equals 543.
5	-	The word "wind" is defined in the text as moving air. It is the correct answer.
6	B	The word "bend" means to move one way or another in the text. The clue is "up and down". The second definition is correct.
7	B,C	The two sets of words that are the same are fast, quicker and goes, moves. The second and third sets are correct. The other sets of words are not the same or similar to each other in meaning. They are not correct.
8	-	The text states that air and water are the materials that sound goes through. Those are the only correct answers.

Question No.	Answer	Detailed Explanation
1	C	The answer is C. When adding or subtracting 10, the only digit that changes is the digit in the tens place unless it is necessary to bundle.
2	A	The answer is A. When adding or subtracting 100,, the only digit that changes is the digit in the hundreds place unless it is necessary to bundle.
3	D	The answer is D. When adding or subtracting 10, the only digit that changes is the digit in the tens place.
4	C	The answer is C. When adding or subtracting 100,, the only digit that changes is the digit in the hundreds place unless it is necessary to bundle.
5	-	The glossary gives the definitions. Rural is country living, urban is city living, and suburban is close to the city living. These are the only correct answers.
6	A	The first answer is correct. In the glossary it states that congestion is something blocked or slowed. If the traffic was blocked or slowed down, people could be late for their jobs. The other answers are not found and are not correct.
7	-	The glossary lists bus, car, truck, subway, bicycle, train and plane. These are the correct answers. They may be in any order.
8	-	Answers will vary. The correct answer should say that it is a person who lives in a community. It can give more details such as anyone living in a certain place, a person living in an area, somebody who lives somewhere, etc.

Question No.	Answer	Detailed Explanation
1	A	The answer is A. The 4 and the 1 are in the tens place, so they have a Value of 40 and 10 and they equal 50. The 3 and 6 are in the ones place And they have a value of 3 and 6 and they equal 9. 50 plus 9 equals 59.
2	B	The answer is B. The 2 and the 1 are in the tens place, so they have a value of 20 and 10 and they equal 30. The 7 and 2 are in the ones place and they have a value of 7 and 2 and they equal 9. 30 plus 9 equals 39.
3	A	The answer is A. The 3 and the 6 are in the tens place, so they have a value 60 and 30 and they equal 90. The 4 and the 7 are in the ones place and They have a value of 1 and 7 and they equal 8. 90 plus 8 equals 98.
4	C	The answer is C. The 4 and 1 are in the tens place and they have a value of 40 and 10 and they equal 50. The 6 and 5 are in the ones place and they have a value of 6 and 5 and they equal 11. 50 plus 11 equals 61.
5	B	The main idea is that "Owls have many characteristics". The second sentence is the correct answer. The others are details and not the main idea. They are not correct.
6	-	The characteristics in the passage are nocturnal, can be pets, and can make loud noises. These should be marked "yes". They do not have a good sense of smell. That one should be marked "no".
7	B	Characteristic and trait mean the same thing. The second sentence is correct. The other words and definitions do not match the characteristic definition. They are not correct.
8	B, C	The second and third answers are correct. The first and fourth answers are not true. They are not correct.

Week 3

Question No.	Answer	Detailed Explanation
1	C	The answer is 231. There are 2 hundred blocks, 3 tens blocks, and 1 one block.
2	C	The answer is C. 8 hundreds, 3 tens, and 9 ones is 839.
3	B	The answer is B. The number 419 has 4 hundreds, 1 ten, and 9 ones.
4	B	We know that 88 tens is equal to $88 \times 10 = 880$. The maximum number of groups of hundred we can get from 880 is 8. Hence, the correct option is B.
5	D	The first, second and third sentences are not found and are not correct. The fourth sentence gives the overall main idea, the pictures and text help you to better understand pulleys and is correct.
6	D	The last sentence clarifies the purpose of the text and is correct. The other sentences are details that support the main idea. They are not correct.
7	-	The objects should be matched as to what the pulleys help each one to do. The first object should be fishing pole, as it helps bring in the fish, the second one should be blinds as it helps to raise or lower, and the third one should be come-along as it helps to move heavy objects. These are the only correct answers.
8	-	Answers will vary. The answer should include that they help you to see the objects and then read the text to understand how the pulleys work in each one to make the work easier.

Week 4

Question No.	Answer	Detailed Explanation
1	A	The answer is A. The line starts at the beginning and ends on 8. The line Measures 8 inches.
2	C	The answer is 7 inches. The line starts on 2 and ends on 9. The difference between 9 and 2 is 7.
3	C	The answer is C. The line starts on 3 and ends on 12. The difference between 12 and 3 is 9.
4	B	The answer is B. The line starts on 7 and ends at 11. The difference between 11 and 7 is 4.
5	B	The second sentence is the point that the author is trying to make. It is correct because it states in the text that signs are important to learn and follow to help you and keep you safe. The first, third, and fourth sentences are details but not the topic. They are not correct.
6	-	The signs are listed as stop sign first, telling you to stop; buckle up sign second, telling you to put on your seat belt; and third danger sign, telling you to stay away from something. These are the only correct answers and correct order.
7	A, B	The first and second sentences are NOT reasons for following signs and are correct. The third and fourth sentences are reasons and are not correct.
8	-	Answers will vary but need to include that signs are important to help keep you safe. The reasons given are to follow stop signs, follow buckle up signs, and danger keep out signs for your safety. Accept all reasonable answers.

Day 2

Question No.	Answer	Detailed Explanation
1	C	The answer is C. If you look at the ruler, 7 centimeters come before 3 inches.
2	A	The answer is A. If you look at the ruler, 3 inches fall in between 7 and 8 centimeters.
3	D	The answer is D. If you look at the ruler, 2 ½ inches comes before 7 centimeters, which means it is less.
4	B	The answer is B. If you look at the ruler, 7 centimeters is closer to 3 inches than it is to 2 inches.
5	C	The third sentence is the best answer as it tells how the reasons support what the author is trying to tell about. The first, second and fourth answers are details. They are not correct.
6	B	The text says that cats have excellent hearing. The second sentence is correct. The other sentences are not correct and not found.
7	-	The text says that cats are called kittens when they are babies, grown boy cats are called Toms and grown girl cats are called Queens. These are the only correct answers but can be in any order.
8	-	Answers will vary but should include that cats can be either left or right handed and most use their right paws.

Week 4

Question No.	Answer	Detailed Explanation
1	A	The answer is A. If you measure the height of an orange it should be CLOSER to 8 centimeters than any other unit. This is an estimate.
2	C	The answer is C. If you measure a fork it should be CLOSER to 6 inches than any other unit. This is an estimate.
3	B	The answer is B. If you measure a door it should be CLOSER to 7 feet than any other unit. This is an estimate.
4	A	The answer is A. If you measure a paperclip it should be CLOSER to 12 centimeters than any other unit. This is an estimate.
5	-	The words should be put in the order of their first letter. The correct answers are apple, banana, carrot, drive, elephant.
6	B	The correct ABC order of these long vowel words would be tail, team, tone, and train. This makes train NOT in the correct order on this list and is the correct answer
7	-	Following the rule of 2 vowels next to each other, the words mail and street have long vowel sounds. They should be marked long vowel. The words bat and box have only one vowel and have the short vowel sound. They should be marked short vowel.
8	-	The vowel combinations in each word are as follows and are the only correct answers. Sneak-ea, goat-oa, trail-ai, clean-ea, and deep-ee.

Day 4

Question No.	Answer	Detailed Explanation
1	D	The answer is D. Rectangle B is 8 cm. Rectangle A is 11 ½ cm. The difference between 11 ½ and 8 is 3 ½.
2	C	The answer is C. Rectangle A is ½ inches. Rectangle B is 10 ½ inches. The difference between 10 ½ and ½ is 10.
3	B	The answer is B. Rectangle B starts on 2 inches and ends on 8 inches, so it is 6 inches in length. Rectangle A starts on 5 inches and ends on 8 inches, so it is 3 inches in length. The difference between 6 and 3 is 3.
4	A	The answer is A. Rectangle A starts on 2 cm and ends on 12 cm, so it is 10 cm in length. Rectangle B starts on 3 cm and ends on 8 cm, so it is 5 cm in length. The difference between 10 cm and 5 cm is 5 cm.
5	A,C,D	The first, third and fourth sentences are found in the story. Giraffes weigh over 2 thousand pounds, they sleep standing up, and can be found in the wild in Africa. These are correct and should be marked. The second sentence is not a fact and is not correct.
6	B	The story states that they can run about 35 miles an hour. The second sentence is correct.
7	-	Answers will vary but should include that giraffes get their water from the leaves they eat. That is why they do not need to drink much water.
8	-	Facts- giraffes can be 3 times taller than people, and males are called bulls, females are called cows. Not facts giraffes eat mice, and they are only found in Africa. These are the way the details should be marked to be correct as found in the story

Question No.	Answer	Detailed Explanation
1	C	The answer is C. You will need to subtract to get the answer. If Brian's string was 36 inches, but now is 12 inches, then he cut off 24 inches because the difference between 36 and 12 is 24.
2	A	The answer is A. You need to add to get the answer. If the cafeteria door is 65 feet from the office door and the office door is 30 from the gym, you need to add those two numbers to get the total feet all the way from the cafeteria, past the office, and to the gym.
3	D	The answer is D. If Lola's 3 pieces of string totals 12 inches and they are the same length then you should add the same number 3 times and get 12. 4 + 4 + 4 equals 12.
4	C	The answer is C. If each ink pen is 4 inches long and there are 5 ink pens, then 4 + 4 + 4 + 4 + 4 = 20.
5	A,B,D	Benjamin Franklin was a Founding Father, author and inventor. The first, second and fourth sentences are found in the selection. They are correct. The third sentence is not and is not correct.
6	-	The correct answers are a. electricity b. Founding Fathers c. 84 d. US Constitution These must be in this order and are the only correct answers found in the text.
7	-	Mr. Franklin was an inventor, scientist, soldier, politician, postmaster, and author. These are the jobs listed in the story but can be in any order.
8	-	Answers will vary but should include that the text about Benjamin Franklin was written to help you learn more about what all he did and how he did things to help the country.

Question No.	Answer	Detailed Explanation
1	D	The answer is D. If you add 20 to 54, then you will get 74.
2	A	The answer is A. Each jump is 5. If you jump 5 times, then it is 20, 25, and 30.
3	B	The answer is B. Each jump is 2. 2 + 2 + 2 = 6, so that is 3 jumps to reach 28 (22 + 6).
4	A	The answer is A. Each jump is 10. 35 + 10 = 45, so you will jump one time from 35 to get to 45.
5	B	The best definition is the second choice, certain areas of the country. The other answers do not define the word regional.
6	-	Answers vary but should include that animals relocate- move to find a place that has the temperature climate the same that they are used to living in.
7	-	The words in the paragraph that help you to understand the word "species" that should b underlined are Many kinds of animals. The other underlined words do not tell about or give you clues for the underlined words.
8	-	The text states that scientists use reports, charts, graphs, and daily monitoring of land in their data. These can be in any order, must be listed to be correct.

Question No.	Answer	Detailed Explanation
1	D	The answer is D. The hour hand is on the six and the minute hand is on the 1, which represents :05.
2	A	The answer is A. The hour hand is on the eleven and the minute hand is on the 3, which represents :15.
3	C	The answer is C. The hour hand is in between the 8 and 9, and the minute hand is on the 6, which represents :30.
4	C	The answer is C. The hour hand is in between the 3 and the 4, and the minute hand is on the 9 which represents :45.
5	-	The correct collective nouns are flock, litter, swarm, and pack. These words describe the group of things in each sentence.
6	-	herd, bunch, flock, swarm
7	A,D	The correct answers are- We looked for the deck of cards, and There was a colony of ants in our garden. These are the only sentences with collective nouns in them.
8	A	The phrase that does NOT have a collective noun in it is the first phrase- ran to the store. It is the correct answer. The other phrases all have collective nouns in them- band, bundle, and bunch. They are incorrect.

Question No.	Answer	Detailed Explanation
1	D	The answer is D. The value of a dime is 10 cent, so three dimes is 30 cents. The value of a penny is 1 cent, so 4 pennies is 4 cents. If you add them together, you get the total of $1.34.
2	A	The answer is A. The value of 2 quarters is 0.50, the value of 3 dimes is 0.30, the value of 4 nickels is 0.20, and the value of 1 penny is 0.01. If you add them together, you get the total of $1.01.
3	C	The answer is C. 3 dollars have a value of 3.00, 4 quarters have a value of 1.00, and 6 pennies have a value of 0.06. If you add them together you get $4.06.
4	B	The answer is B. 6 quarters have a value of 1.50, 3 dimes have a value of 0.30, and 2 nickels have a value of 0.10. If you add them together, you get $1.90.
5	-	The words should be marked as follows- elephant and slipper are nouns, as they name things; little and fuzzy are adjectives, as they tell about the nouns; walking and running are verbs, as they tell actions; and really and quickly are adverbs, as they tell more about the verbs. These are the correct answers
6	B,C	A complete sentence must have a subject and a predicate. The first and fourth sentences do not have subjects. They are not correct. The second and third sentences are correct. They both have subjects and predicates. Margie and I love to go hiking in the woods. Tracy is happy that he has a new little baby brother.
7	-	The first phrase-ran a long way home is missing a subject, the second phrase- My friends and I is missing a predicate, the third phrase- Grandma and Grandpa is missing a predicate and the fourth phrase- skipping in the rain is missing a subject. These are the only correct answers.
8	-	To use each verb one time, the only correct answers are: a. draw, b. follow, c. ran, d. bake, e. see.

Question No.	Answer	Detailed Explanation
1	C	The answer is C because on the line plot 4 and 6 does not have an x (any data plotted on that number).
2	A	The answer is A. Each x represents 2 pieces of ribbon.
3	C	The answer is C. Each x represent 2 pieces of ribbon. 4 Xs is 8 pieces of ribbon.
4	B	The answer is B. Each x counts for 2 pieces of ribbon. Kim has 4 pieces that is 3 inches, 4 pieces that are 5 inches, and 2 pieces that are 7 inches. There are 10 pieces of ribbon that are 3 inches or greater.
5	-	By changing the "f" in each word to a "v" and adding "es" the following words are correct- wolves, shelves, leaves, knives, and elves.
6	-	By changing the "y" to "i" and adding "es", the new plural words are butterflies, flies, stories, and babies. These are the only correct words.
7	-	The correct matches for singular to plural are box to boxes, bench to benches, wish to wishes, tomato to tomatoes, and potato to potatoes.
8	-	The correct plurals for each sentence are mice, people, geese, and feet. The other choices are not the correct plural form of the nouns.

Question No.	Answer	Detailed Explanation
1	A	The answer is A. August only had 1 birthday.
2	D	The answer is D. The graph stops in between 2 and 4.
3	B	The answer is B. June has 10 birthdays.
4	B	The answer is B. There are currently 7 employees with December birthdays. If a new employee has a December birthday, then it will be 8 birthdays.
5	-	The reflexive pronouns in each sentence are themselves, myself, herself, and ourselves. These are the only correct answers.
6	-	The correct answers are for sentence #1 subject is I and reflexive pronoun is myself, sentence #2 subject is She and reflexive pronoun is herself, sentence #3 subject is We and reflexive pronoun is ourselves.
7	-	The correct answer choices are: a. ourselves, as it reflects the subject We. b. herself as it reflects the subject She. c. themselves as it reflects the subject They. d. himself as it reflects the subject He.
8	B	The sentence that does not have a reflexive pronoun is the second sentence- Sarah and Tammy played the piano. The other sentences all have reflexive pronouns himself, himself, and themselves.

Question No.	Answer	Detailed Explanation
1	C	The answer is C. A rectangle has four sides.
2	B	The answer is B. A square has four equal sides.
3	B	The answer is B. The face of a cube is a square.
4	C	The answer is C. The pentagon has 5 sides.
5	B,D	The correct sentences that give information about what verbs do in a sentence are the second and fourth sentences. Verbs tell the action in a sentence. Verbs are a part of the predicate. The first and third sentences are not correct.
6	-	Using the text on irregular verbs, the following is the only correct answer- verb is changed to a new word or stays the same in present and past tense.
7	A,D,F,G	The correct past tense irregular verbs in the list are: sat, ate, hid, and told. The others are present tense verbs.
8	-	The correct past tense irregular verbs for the sentences are a. ran b. went c. saw d. taught

Day 2

Question No.	Answer	Detailed Explanation
1	C	The answer is C. Columns go up and down and rows go across. C has 4 columns and 3 rows
2	D	The answer is D. Columns go up and down and rows go across. D has 5 rows and 4 columns.
3	A	The answer is A. Columns go up and down and rows go across. A has 5 rows and 5 columns.
4	C	The answer is C. Columns go up and down and rows go across. C has 7 columns and 6 rows.
5	-	The phrases that are not complete sentences are "Mary and Jane want. to go to the store" and "Mary asked her mother. for some money." The other sentences are complete and have both subjects and verbs.
5.1	-	The correct sentences must be- Mary and Jane want to go to the store. Mary asked her mother for some money. These are the only correct answers.
6	-	The complete sentences from the story are- They got ready. Her mother gave her $2. Jane got $5 from her dad. These are the only correct answers but may be in any order.
7	-	The correct matches are- the beautiful ponies were fun to ride, Roberto and Miguel love to play football, The chicken soup was good to eat, and She brushed her hair. No other answers are correct.
8	-	The correct matches are sped down the hill to The racecar, rode her bike up the road to Betty, started ringing when the fire began to alarm, and broke as it fell to the floor to The dish. These are the only right answers because the question states that each can only be used one time.

Question No.	Answer	Detailed Explanation
1	C	The answer is C. Halves must be equal parts and C has two parts that are the same size.
2	A	The answer is A. Thirds must be equal parts and A has three parts that are the same size.
3	B	The answer is B. Fourths must be equal parts and B has four parts that are the same size.
4	A	The answer is A. There are three equal parts and one out of three parts are shaded.
5	-	The correct proper nouns in the sentences are 1. Sarah, 2. Dallas, Texas, 3. Valentine's Day, and 4. John, Skipper, Saturday. These all must be highlighted as they name particular people, places, holidays, and days of the week.
6	-	The words that should be capitalized and name a particular product are Cheerios cereal, Skippy peanut butter, and Kraft cheese. The word popcorn should not be capitalized as it does not name a particular product brand.
7	A,C,D	The correct answers are the first, third and fourth choices. Dear Mayor, - Dearest Grandma, - and Respectfully, - they use the comma correctly. The second answer does not use the comma correctly, as it should be after you – not after Thank. It is not correct.
8	-	a. should not = shouldn't b. is not = isn't c. did not = didn't

Day 4

Question No.	Answer	Detailed Explanation
1	D	The answer is D. Jimmy exercised for 36 minutes on Monday. To find out how long he exercised on Tuesday, you must add 36 and 12. 36 plus 12 equals 48. 36 (Monday) plus 48 (Tuesday) equals 84.
2	87	The answer is 87. You are finding the difference between the grade this week and last week. To find a difference, you must subtract. 98 minus 11 equals 87.
3	-	The first problem should be solved using subtraction because you are taking away the books read to find out the books that have not been read. The second problem is solved using addition because you are adding the books Lisa bought to the books she already had.
4	-	26 plus 19 equals 45, so that is the amount that Brittney and Joshua have saved. You should subtract to find the difference between the money Brittney has saved and Joshua has saved. The difference between 26 and 19 is 7. The video game costs 59 dollars and they already have 45. You should subtract to find out how much more money they need to buy the game. 59 minus 45 equals 14.
5	A,C,D	The correct answers are Easter, Memorial Day, Valentine's Day. They are holidays. Eggs and Presents are not correct as they are not holidays.
6	B	The correct sentence is- Mary and her mother made cupcakes for Veteran's Day. The other sentences have holidays in them, but they are not correct as they are not capitalized.
7	brand	The words that should be capitalized and marked in the box are Ford, Amazon, M & M's, and Coca Cola. They are product brand names. The other words truck, dog food, candy and store are not product names and should be marked do not capitalize.
8	A,B	The 2 sentences that use product brand names correctly are- Most people like to eat Lay's chips. – He drove a bright shiny Toyota truck. The other sentences have product names, but they are not brand names and are not capitalized, so they are not correct.

Question No.	Answer	Detailed Explanation
1	B,C&E	The answer are B, C, & E , because they all equal 4 when they are subtracted.
2	7	The answer is 7. 7 + 7 = 14.
3		14 + 3= 17 Does not equal to 12 11 + 1= 12 Equals to 12 20 - 8= 12 Equals to 12 18 - 6= 12 Equals to 12 2 + 10= 12 Equals to 12
4		15 + 2 = 17 19 - 7 = 12 2 + 5 = 7 18 - 15 = 3
5	A,C,D	The correct answers are Dear Calvin, - Dearest Grandmother, - To Whom It May Concern, - the other answers are not correct as they do not use the comma at the end of the salutation.
6	-	The corrections should be that a comma is added after Daddy and after again. These are the only correct answers.
7	D	The only correct answer is Dear Aunt Bea, as it has the correct use of the comma. The other answers are not correct as they do not have the comma placed at the end of the salutation.
8	-	The salutations that should be fixed are To the President, and Dear Eddie, - the others have the correct use of the comma. These are the only correct answers.

Question No.	Answer	Detailed Explanation
1	C,D & E	The answer are C, D, & E. Even numbers have the digit 0, 2, 4, 6 or 8 in the ones place.
2	A,D & E	The answer are A, D, & E. An even and an odd number will always equal an odd number. Two even numbers will always equal and even number. Two odd numbers will always equal an odd number.
3	19	The answer is 19. You can draw out 9 pairs and one additional. When you count the 9 pairs you get 18 and when you add one more you get 19. It should be understood the answer will be an odd number because they are not all paired.
4	Odd Even Odd Even	13 (7+6) is odd, 16 (8+8) is even, 7 (4+3) is odd, 6 (2+4) is even. Even numbers are divisible by two and always has a pair. Odd numbers have visually one left over.
5	-	Following the rules given in the information, taking out the "a" in "are" and replacing it with an ' and taking out the "i" in "is" and replacing it with an ' make the new contractions. The correct contractions to make are' they're, we're, she's, he's, and you're. These are the only answers.
6	B, C	The two sentences that have contractions in them are – We aren't going to go shopping until Friday. They're happy to go on vacation. They are the correct answers. The other sentences do not have contractions in them and are not correct.
7	-	The correct answers are -aren't, haven't, didn't, and isn't. They are the only answers when the not is the second word and the letter "o" is left out and 'put in its place.
8	C	The only correct answer is the third sentence. The firemen won't let the fire spread. It has the contraction "won't" in it for will not.

Day 2

Question No.	Answer	Detailed Explanation
1	A & B	The answers are A & B. The arrays can be represented as an addition equation by adding the number of circles in the row (5) as many times as there are rows (3). The array can also be represented by multiplying the number of rows (3) by how many circles are in each row (5).
2	A & D	The answers are A & D. The arrays can be represented as an addition equation by adding the number of circles in the row (2) as many times as there are rows (5). The array can also be represented by multiplying the number of rows (5) by how many circles are in each row (2).
3	20	The answer is 20. You should draw an array of 5 rows and 4 in each row. You can use an addition sentence 4 + 4 + 4 + 4 + 4 = 20.
4	-	The answers can be found by using addition equations, multiplication equations, and/or counting.
5	B, C, D, E	The correct answers are the words back, rack, stick, and flick. They have a short vowel and end in the "k" sound spelled "ck". The other words do not follow the rule and are not correct.
6	-	The words that should be marked YES are play, stay, and away. They follow the rule of "ay" at the end of the word. The words that should be marked NO are bake and story. These do not follow the rule.
7	-	The words with long "e" are We, tree in sentence 1, eat, piece in sentence 2, Please in sentence 3, and freeze in sentence 4. These are the only correct answers that follow the long "e" rules.
8	B, D, E	The correct answers are Beef, Sleep, and Meat. They follow the long "e" patterns. The other words are short "e" and are not correct.

Question No.	Answer	Detailed Explanation
1	B	The answer is B. 58 has 5 tens and 8 ones, but it does not have hundreds.
2	B	The answer is B. 340 does not have ones.
3	10	The answer is 10. It takes 10 tens to make one hundred. Students can use place value blocks, count by 10, repeated addition, etc to figure out the answer if they do not already know this concept.
4		8 ones, 3 tens, 5 hundreds --> 538 8 hundreds, 5 tens, 3 ones --> 853 8 tens, 3 ones, 5 hundreds --> 583 5 ones, 3 hundreds, 8 tens --> 385
5	B	The guide words that would be on the top of the page in a dictionary where the word – giraffe- would be found are - "germ great". The word giraffe would fall between these words in ABC order. The second answer is correct. It would not with the other guide words. They are not correct.
6	B	The correct answer is -Excited- eager, enthusiastic, anticipating emotions. This is the only correct answer. The other definitions of words- explosive, and skinny- do not make sense in the sentence.
7	B, C	The 2 words that are not spelled correctly and need to be looked up in the dictionary to correct the spelling are- forgeting, and childran. They should be marked. The other words- happy and complete are spelled correctly and do not need to be checked.
8	B, C, E	The topics that would be found in an online encyclopedia are -Rainforest, Trees, and Cats. They are correct. The words funny and walking might not be in an online encyclopedia or would not contain as much information and are not correct.

Day 4

Question No.	Answer	Detailed Explanation
1	B	The answer is B. 80 tens equals 800. 800 equals 8 hundreds.
2	C	The answer is 3. 10 blocks equal a hundred. You can bundle 3 groups of ten from the blocks above.
3	7	The answer is 7. 6 hundred blocks represents 6 hundreds. 10 ten block represent 1 hundred. 6 hundreds + 1 hundred = 7 hundreds (700).
4		Blake is incorrect. 700 ones is equivalent to 70 tens. There are 10 ones in every ten. There are 100 ones in one hundred. So 700 ones is 7 hundreds. There are 10 tens in every hundred. 70 tens is 7 hundreds. That is why 700 ones is equivalent to 70 tens.
5	D	The story setting is at Noe's house. That is the only correct answer. The other answers are not found and are not correct.
6	-	The characters in the story are Noe and Kevin. They can be listed in any order to be correct.
7	-	Answers will vary but must include that the problem was the boys needed to fill with air the tires on their bikes.
8	A, B	The best ideas would be the first and second sentences. You could get the materials and make the sandwich while you were talking about it. You could pass out notes to the class, so they could follow along. The other sentences would not be correct.

Question No.	Answer	Detailed Explanation
1	D	The answer is D.
2		310, 410, 510, 610, 710, 810 --> 100s 305, 310, 315, 320, 325, 330 --> 5s 715, 725, 735, 745, 755, 765 --> 10s 400, 405, 410, 415, 420, 425 --> 5s
3		(see table below)

535	545	555	**565**	75
803	**813**	**823**	**833**	843
225	325	425	**525**	**625**
800	**810**	**820**	830	**840**

Question No.	Answer	Detailed Explanation
4		Ted is not correct. When you start at a number and count by 10s the number in the ones place does not change. If you start counting by 10s from the number 18, then every number in the pattern will end in 8.
5	-	The informal names are Mother, Classmate, Best Friend, and Grandma. The formal names are Mayor, and President. These are the only correct answers.
6	-	The correct answers are a. informal (talking to a friend), b. formal (invite to a judge), c. formal (formal invitation), d. informal (friends), e. formal (speaking to the President).
7	A, D	The 2 sentences that show informal use of English are "Mom, I am hungry!" and "Yeah, we won the game!" They are correct. The other 2 sentences are formal use and are not correct.
8	-	Formal

Question No.	Answer	Detailed Explanation
1	C	The answer is C. When numbers are in different forms, then you should convert each number to standard from before comparing. When comparing numbers, you can begin in the highest places and compare the digits in that place. If the digits are the same, you can move to the next lower place.
2	A, B & D	The answers are A, B, & D. When numbers are in different forms, then you should convert each number to standard from before comparing. When comparing numbers, you can begin in the highest places and compare the digits in that place. If the digits are the same, you can move to the next lower place.
3	342	342
4		$459 < 495$ $233 > 200 + 30 + 1$ $700 + 70 > 700 + 7$ $200 + 40 = 240$
5	-	The correct answers are a. unhappy- not happy, b. unopened- not opened, c. unable- not able, d. unknown- not known. There are no other answers.
6	B	The correct answer is B. She untied her shoelaces. In this sentence, the word "untied" has the prefix "un" which means not.
7	-	The correct answers are a. reread- read again, b. replay – play again, c. redo – do again. There are no other answers.
8	-	The first sentence has the word "preschool" in it and should be underlined. The second sentence has the word "preheat" in it and should be highlighted. These are the only correct answers.

Day 2

Question No.	Answer	Detailed Explanation
1	A,B & D	The answers are A, B, & D. 78 minus 10 equals 68. 34 plus 34 equals 68. 22 plus 46 equals 68.
2	C & D	The answers are C & D. 65 minus 42 equals 23. 3 plus 20 equals 23.
3	21	The answer is 21. The answer can be found by subtracting 75 minus 54 equals 21. So that means that 54 plus 21 equals 75. So x equals 21.
4		$23 + \mathbf{18} = 41$ $62 - \mathbf{32} = 30$ $48 - \mathbf{27} = 21$
5	-	The correct adjectives are purple, second-grade, yellow bright, funny, grumpy old, and good. They tell about each of the nouns in the phrases
6	A	The first sentence has 3 adjectives in it. The pretty little lady was looking for her tiny kitten. The first sentence is correct. The other sentences have adverbs and do not have 3 adjectives.
7	C	The adjective that makes sense in the sentence is fluffy. It is the only correct answer. The words loudly, and well are adverbs and do not make sense. The words first-grade are adjectives, but do not make sense. They are incorrect.
8	-	The correct adjectives are good, huge, orange, and sweet. The other words are not adjectives and do not make sense. They are not correct.

Question No.	Answer	Detailed Explanation
1	D	The answer is D. You can take 42 + 11 (53) and 14 + 9 (23) and add them together to get the answer. 53
2	D	The answer is D. 21 + 24 + 55 + 2 = 102. If you add 21 + 55, the answer is 76. If you add 21 + 2, the answer is 23. 76 plus 23 equals 99, so it is NOT another way to add the equation.
3	122	The answer is 122.
4		28 + 17 + 44 + 22 = 111 39 + 18 + 24 + 29 = 110 6 + 68 + 12 + 25 = 111
5	-	The words that should be underlined are broke, iron, and cave. Each word should be highlighted 2 times to be correct.
6	-	The correct answers are 1. handle, 2. mind, 3. stare, 4. flower, 5. mind, and 6. flour. These are the only correct answers.
7	-	The words that rhyme are scout with about, believe with relieve, sing with ring, and fox with box. These are the only correct answers.
8	-	The correct answers are piece, peace and knows, nose. These are the only answers where the words sound the same in each row and mean something different

Day 4

Question No.	Answer	Detailed Explanation
1		The answer is B. In order to find the missing part (addend), you can subtract the other addend from the whole sum. $309 - 109 = 200$. So x has a value of 200 because 109 plus 200 equals 309.
2		The answer is D. To find the missing part, you can subtract the whole difference from the minuend. 385 minus 300 equals 85, so x has a value of 85. 385 minus 85 equals 300.
3		The answer is 426.
4		When we add 124 and 179 we get 303 572-259 gives 313 491-189 gives 302 and 209 +103 is 312
5	D	These are correct because they give the meaning of the underlined word in each sentence.
5.1	A	
5.2	B	
6		The correct answers are careful, hopeless, breakable, and thankful. These are the only words that can be made with the new endings added.
7		The correct answers are- able for comfortable, -less for hopeless, -ful for respectful, and -ful for playful. These are the only correct answers.
8		The correct root word for respectful, respected, and respects is respect. The correct root word for careless, careful, and caring is care. The correct root word for playful, played, and playing is play. The correct root word for breakable, breaking, and breaks is break. These are the only correct answers.

Week 8

Question No.	Answer	Detailed Explanation
1	C	The answer is C. When adding or subtracting 100,, the only digit that changes is the digit in the hundreds place unless it is necessary to bundle.
2	A & D	The answers are A & D. When adding or subtracting 100, the only digit that changes is the digit in the hundreds place unless it is necessary to bundle.
3	1,009	The answer is 1,009. When adding or subtracting 100, the only digit that changes is the digit in the hundreds place unless it is necessary to bundle.
4		546 is 10 more than 536 297 is 100 less than 397 891 is 10 less than 901 1000 is 100 more than 900
5	-	The correct compound words are hamburger, popcorn, milkshake, butterfly and toothbrush. They must be in this order to be correct.
6	-	The correct compound words in ABC order are doorbell, football, homework and weekend. They must be in order to be correct.
7	-	Sentence 1- horseback is the correct answer to highlight. Sentence 2- skateboard is the correct answer to highlight. Sentence 3- Grandma is the correct answer to highlight. Sentence 4- Someone is the correct answer to highlight. Sentence 5- Watermelon is the correct answer to highlight. These are the compound words in the sentences.
8	C	The compound word that would be used if talking about something to carry books in is backpack. It is correct. The other compound words do not make sense or answer the questions.

Question No.	Answer	Detailed Explanation
1	D	The answer is D. 213 should have 2 hundred blocks, 1 ten block. And 3 ones.
2	C	The answer is C. There is 1 hundred block, 7 ten blocks, and 2 ones.
3	152	The answer is 152. There are 15 tens. 10 of them will be bundled together to make 1 hundred. There are 5 tens left. 5 tens is equivalent to 50. There are 2 ones. 1 hundred, 5 tens, 2 ones is 152.
4		13 tens = 130 and 200 ones = 200. Therefore, $130+200 = 330 > 300$ 14 tens = 140 and 150 ones = 150. Therefore, $140+150 = 290 < 300$ 27 tens = 270 and 3 ones = 3. Therefore, $270+3 = 273 < 300$ 20 tens = 200 and 15 ones = 15. Therefore, $200+15 = 215 < 300$
5	-	The word that is weaker is afraid and the stronger word is frightened. This is the only correct answer as afraid gives a feeling of being scared, but frightened gives more of an emotion.
6	-	The correct answers for the sentences are: a. gorgeous as it is a more detailed meaning for very pretty b. frightened as it is a more detailed meaning for very scared c. awful as it is a more detailed meaning for very bad d. gigantic as it is a more detailed meaning for very big.
7	-	yes, play, closed, there
8	-	The correct word matches are hot to cold, happy to sad, short to tall, fast to slow, left to right and on to off. These are the only correct answers

Day 2

Question No.	Answer	Detailed Explanation
1	A, B, D & E	The answers are A, B, D, & E. They all represent 7 inches. The difference of 7-0 is 7. The difference of 10 − 3 = 7. The difference between 12 − 5 = 7. The difference between 9 − 2 = 7.
2	C	The answer is C because the difference between 14 and 5 is 9.
3	17cm	The answer is 17cm. You should add how long it is to the place that Kaylie started on.
4		The difference between 11 and 2 is 9. The difference between 11 ½ and 4 ½ is 7. The difference between 11 and 9 is 2. The difference 7 and 2 is 5.
5	-	The correct answers are rainbow to - bright, colorful half-circle in the sky, pot of gold; puppy to- baby dog, cute 4-legged pet; computer to- desktop, laptop, technology tool, and friend to- buddy, pal, companion. These are the only correct answers.
6	-	a. playground b. laugh c. recess d. shout
7	-	The words that must be marked farm animals are cow, horse, and chicken. The words that must be marked indoor pet animals are dog and hamster. The words that must be marked wild or jungle animals are elephant, lion, giraffe, and bear. These are the only correct answers.
8	B	The best answer is soft, cuddly, huggable. The other answer does not describe a stuffed animal. It is not correct.

Day 3

Question No.	Answer	Detailed Explanation
1	B	The answer is B. If you look at the ruler, the centimeters are at the top. The line begins at 0 centimeters and ends at 8 centimeters.
2	A	The correct answer is A. If you look at the ruler, the line is very close to 3 Inches. The inches are on the bottom of the ruler.
3	2 cm	The answer is 2 centimeters. The pencil was 10 and if it is now 8, the difference between 10 – 8 is 2.
4		9 centimeters is shorter than 3/12 inches --> False 4 1/2 inches is between 11 and 12 centimeters--> True 5 inches is closer to 13 centimeters than 12 centimeters--> True
5	B	The verbs that are similar (related) to each other and describe what you could do with a ball are - toss, drop, throw, hurl, pitch, bounce. That is the correct answer. The other list of verbs describes eating or drinking and is not correct.
6	-	The correct matches of verbs that are related or similar are tidy, clean to neat; weep, sob to cry; tired, drowsy to sleepy; chat, talk to speak. These are the only correct matches.
7	-	The correct answer is excellent as it is related to the adjective good. The boys did an excellent job on their project.
8	B	The correct answer is the second sentence. She giggled when she saw the funny face on the clown. The verb that is related to laugh in the sentence is giggled. The other sentences do not have related verbs and are not correct.

Day 4

Question No.	Answer	Detailed Explanation
1	A	The answer is A. If you measure a sheet of paper it should be CLOSER to 18 centimeters than any other unit. This is an estimate.
2	D	The answer is D. If you measure the height of a refrigerator it should be CLOSER to 2 meters than any other unit. This is an estimate.
3	12	12 inches
4		The height of a birthday candle is about 2 Centimeters The height of a chair is about 1 Meter The height of a box of cereal is about 12 Inches The height of a vacuum cleaner is about 4 Feet
5	-	The correct answers are deep, dark. They describe the woods in the story. They are the only correct answers.
6	-	The correct answers are frightened, scared. They tell about being afraid. They are the only correct answers.
7	C, D, E	The correct answers that tell how George and Timothy talked in the story are replied, said, shouted. These are the words used in the conversation and are the only correct answers. The other words answered and spoke are not found in the story. They are not correct.
8	-	Answer may vary.

Question No.	Answer	Detailed Explanation
1	C	The answer is C. Rectangle B is 9 ½ inches and Rectangle A is 10 inches. The difference between 10 and 9 ½ is ½ .
2	B	The answer is B. Rectangle A is 8 cm. Rectangle B is 12 cm. The difference between 12 and 8 is 4 cm.
3	2 ½ inches	Rectangle B is 2 inches. Rectangle A 4 ½ inches. The difference between 4 ½ and 2 is 2 ½ .
4		Row 1: Line A is 1 inch longer than Line B Row 2: Line A is 6 cm shorter than Line B Row 3: Line B is 4 inches shorter than Line A Row 4: Line A and B are the same length
5	D	It tells or informs you about things.
6	B	The topic sentence in the writing is- We see weather changes along with new plant and animal life in the Spring. This sentence tells what the writing will be about. The other sentences give details but do not tell the most and are not correct.
7	A, D, E	The correct answer for facts in the writing about Spring are- animals have babies, flowers bloom and leaves grow, and weather is cooler. The other details are not found and are not correct.
8	D	The best concluding statement for the writing is- Spring brings cooler weather and new life for animals and plants.

STOP! IN THE NAME OF EDUCATION: PREVENT SUMMER LEARNING LOSS WITH 7 SIMPLE STEPS

Summer Learning loss is defined as "a loss of knowledge and skills . . . most commonly due to . . . . extended breaks [during the summertime] " (from edglossary.org/learning-loss). Many teachers have certainly had the experience of taking the first month of school not only to introduce his or her rules and procedures to the class but also to get the kids back "up to speed" with thinking, remembering what they've learned . . . and in many cases, reviewing previous content. With a traditional school calendar, then, this can mean that up to 10% of the school year is spent playing catch-up.

What's a parent to do? Fortunately, there are some simple steps you can take with your child to help your son or daughter both enjoy the summer and keep those all-important skills honed and fresh:

(1) Read!

Research supports the relationship between independent reading and student achievement, so simply having your child read daily will make a positive difference. Check out the following sources to find books that your child will want to dive into: your public library, local bookstores, online stores (Amazon, Barnes and Noble, half.com, etc.), and yard sales (if the family hosting the sale has children a bit older than your own, you stand a good chance of scoring discarded books that are a perfect match for your son or daughter's reading level).

(2) Write!

Have your child write letters to out-of-town friends and family, or write postcards while on vacation. A summer journal is another way to document summer activities. For the artistic or tech-savvy child, you may choose to create a family scrapbook with captions (consider the online options at Shutterfly, Mixbook, and Smilebox). Not only will you preserve this summer's memories, but your child will also continue to practice his or her writing skills! (See Summer is Here! Ideas to Keep Your Child's Writing Skills Sharp for more writing ideas.)

(3) Do the Math!

Think of ways your child can incorporate math skills into daily activities: have a yard sale, and put your child in charge of the cash box; help younger ones organize a lemonade stand (to practice salesmanship and making change). Or simply purchase a set of inexpensive flash cards to practice basic facts while waiting in line or on a long car ride. There's even a host of free online games that will keep your child's math skills sharp.

(4) "Homeschool" Your Child

Keeping your child's skills fresh doesn't have to cost a fortune: check out some of the Lumos Learning workbooks and online resources (at lumoslearning.com/store), and your child can work through several exercises each day. Even as little as twenty minutes a day can yield positive results, and it's easy to work in a small block of time here and there. For instance, your child can work in the book during a car ride, right before bedtime, etc. Or, simply make this part of your child's morning routine. For example: wake up, eat breakfast, complete chores, and then work in the workbook for 20 minutes. With time, you can make this a natural habit.

(5) Go Back-to-School Shopping (For a Great Summer School Learning Experience)

Check out offerings from the big names (think Sylvan, Huntington, Mathnasium, and Kumon), and also consider local summer schools. Some school districts and local colleges provide learning programs: research the offerings on-line for more information regarding the available options in your area.

(6) Take a Hike . . . Go Camping!

But "camp" doesn't always involve pitching a tent in the great outdoors. Nowadays, there are camps for every interest: sports camps, art camp, music camp, science camp, writing camp . . . the possibilities are endless! With a quick Internet search, you'll be able to turn up multiple options that will appeal to your son or daughter. And even if these camps aren't "academic", the life skills and interpersonal experiences are certain to help your child succeed in the "real world". For example, working together as a cast to put on a summer theater production involves memorizing lines, cooperation, stage crew coordination, and commitment – all skills that can come in handy when it comes to fostering a good work ethic and the ability to collaborate with others.

(7) Get tutored

Many teachers offer tutoring services throughout the summer months, either for individuals or small groups of students. Even the most school-averse student tends to enjoy the personal attention of a former teacher in a setting outside of the classroom. Plus, a tutor can tailor his or her instruction to pinpoint your child's needs – so you can maximize the tutoring sessions with the skills and concepts your child needs the most help with.

Of course, you don't need to do all seven steps to ensure that your child maintains his or her skills. Just following through with one or two of these options will go a long way toward continued learning, skills maintenance, and easing the transition to school when summer draws to a close.

SUMMER READING: QUESTIONS TO ASK THAT PROMOTE COMPREHENSION

As mentioned in our "Beating Summer Academic Loss" article, students are at risk of losing academic ground during the summer months, especially with respect to their reading level, spelling, and vocabulary. One of the best ways to prevent this "brain drain" for literacy is to have your son or daughter read each day during the summer break.

Better yet, you can promote these all-important skills and participate in your child's summer reading by engaging in active dialogue with your son or daughter. Below are several questions and ideas for discussion that will promote comprehension, recall, and critical thinking skills. In addition, these questions reflect several of the Common Core standards – which underpin the curriculum, instruction and standardized testing for most school districts. Of course, the standards vary by grade level, but some of the common themes that emerge in these standards are: citing evidence, summarizing, and making inferences.

• Citing evidence

Simply put, citing evidence involves going back into the text (book, magazine, newspaper, etc.) and finding "proof" to back up an answer, opinion, or assertion. For instance, you could ask your child, "Did you enjoy this book?" and then follow up that "yes" or "no" response with a "Why?" This requires the reader to provide details and examples from the story to support his or her opinion. For this particular question, then, your child may highlight plot events he or she liked, character attributes, writing style, and even genre (type of book) as evidence. Challenge for older students: Ask your child to go back into the text and find a direct quote to support an opinion or answer.

• Summarizing

For nonfiction pieces, this may involve being able to explain the 5W's – who, what, where, when, why (and how). For literature, ask your child to summarize the story elements, including: the setting, characters, main conflict or problem, events, resolution, and theme/lesson/moral. If your child can do this with specificity and accuracy, there's a very good chance that he or she comprehended the story. Challenge for older students: Ask your child to identify more complex story elements, such as the climax, rising action, and falling action.

• Making inferences

Making an inference is commonly referred to as "reading between the lines." That is, the reader can't find the answer to a question directly in the text but instead must synthesize or analyze information to come to a conclusion. To enhance these higher-level thinking skills, ask your child to describe the main character's personality, describe how a character changed by the end of a novel, or detail how the setting influenced the story's plot. Challenge for older students: Have the reader compare and contrast two or more characters to highlight similarities and differences in personality, actions, etc.

 Of course, if you read the same book that your child reads, you'll be able to come up with even more detailed questions – and also know if your child truly understood the reading based on his or her answers! But even if you don't get a chance to read what your child does, simply asking some of these questions not only helps your child's reading skills but also demonstrates an interest in your child – and his or her reading.

BEATING THE BRAIN DRAIN THROUGH LITERACY: WEBINAR RECAP WITH PRINTABLE ACTIVITY SHEET

Lumos Learning conducted webinar on "Beating the Brain Drain Through Literacy." During this webinar, we provided the students with several ideas for keeping their literacy skills sharp in the summertime.

Here's a handy chart with the ideas from the webinar, ready for you to post on your refrigerator. Let your child pick and choose the activities that appeal to him or her. Of course, reading should be nonnegotiable, but the list below provides alternatives for reluctant readers – or for those who just don't enjoy reading a traditional fiction novel. The first set of activities touch upon ideas that reinforce writing skills, while the second half addresses reading skills. There is also room on the chart to date or check off activities your child has completed.

Skill Area	Activity	Completed this activity	Notes for parents
Writing skills, spelling, and/or vocabulary	Keep a journal (things you do, places you go, people you meet)		Even though journals work on spelling skills, be sure your child understands that spelling "doesn't count". Most children like to keep their journals private, so they don't need to worry about perfect skills or that someone else is going to read/grade what they wrote.
	Start a blog		Enable privacy settings to keep viewers limited to friends and family. Check out WordPress, Squarespace, and Quillpad to begin blogging.
	Get published		The following places publish student work: The Clairmont Review, CyberKids, Creative Kids Magazine, New Moon, and The Young Writer's Magazine.
	Write letters		Have your child write or type letters, postcards, and emails to friends and family members.
	Take part in a family movie night		Watch movies that are thought-provoking to elicit interesting post-movie discussions. Other good bets are movies that are based on a book (read the book first and compare the two).
	Organize a family game night		Choose word games to work on spelling and vocabulary skills (examples: Scrabble, Boggle, and Hangman).
Reading skills: fluency, comprehension, critical thinking, decoding skills, inferencing, etc.	Pick up a good book!		Places to find/buy/borrow books include: your public library, ebooks, yard sales, book stores, your child's school library (if it's open during the summer), and borrowed books from friends and family members.
	Read materials that aren't "books"…		Ideas include: karaoke lyrics, cereal boxes, newspapers, magazines for kids, billboards, close captioning, and audio books.
	Compete! Enter a reading challenge		Scholastic Reading hosts a competition called "Reading Under the Stars" to break a world record for minutes read. Barnes and Noble gives students the opportunity to earn one free book with "Imagination's Destination" reading challenge.

Note: Reading just six books over the summer can maintain — and sometimes even increase! — your child's reading level. Not sure if the book is appropriate for your child's reading level? Use the five-finger rule: have your son/daughter read a page of a book. Each time your child encounters a word that is unfamiliar or unknown, he or she holds up a finger. If your child holds up more than five fingers on a given page, that book is probably too difficult.

However, there are some books that a child will successfully tackle if it's high-interest to him or her. Keep in mind that reading levels are a guide (as is the five-finger rule), and some children may exceed expectations...so don't hold your child back if he or she really wants to read a particular book (even if it may appear to be too challenging).

Remember, if students do some of these simple activities, they can prevent the typical four to six weeks of learning loss due to the "summer slide." And since spelling, vocabulary and reading skills are vulnerable areas, be sure to encourage your child to maintain his or her current literacy level...it will go a long way come September!

SUMMER IS HERE! KEEP YOUR CHILD'S WRITING SKILLS SHARP WITH ONLINE GAMES

Like Reading and math, free online activities exist for all subjects... and writing is no exception. Check out the following free interactive writing activities, puzzles, quizzes and games that reinforce writing skills and encourage creativity:

Primary Level (K-2nd Grade)

Story Writing Game

In this game, the child fills in the blanks of a short story. The challenge is for the storyteller to choose words that fit the kind of story that has been selected. For example, if the child chooses to tell a ghost story, then he or she must select words for each blank that would be appropriate for a scary tale. http://www.funenglishgames.com/writinggames/story.html

Opinions Quiz for Critical Thinking

Practice developing logical reasons to support a thesis with this interactive activity. Students read the stated opinion, such as, "We should have longer recess because..." The child must then select all of the possible reasons from a list that would support the given statement. The challenge lies with the fact that each statement may have more than one possible answer, and to receive credit, the student must select all correct responses. This game is best suited for older primary students. http://www.netrover.com/~kingskid/Opinion/opinion.html

Interactives: Sequence

Allow your child to practice ordering events with this interactive version of the fairy tale, Cinderella. The child looks at several pictures from the story and must drag them to the bottom of the screen to put the events in chronological order. When the player mouses over each scene from the story, a sentence describing the image appears and is read aloud to the student. Once the events are in order, the student can learn more about the plot and other story elements with the accompanying tutorials and lessons. http://www.learner.org/interactives/story/sequence.html

WEBINAR "CLIFF NOTES" FOR BEATING SUMMER ACADEMIC LOSS: AN INFORMATIVE GUIDE TO PARENTS

The "Summer Slide"

First, it's important to understand the implications of "summer slide" – otherwise known as summer learning loss. Research has shown that some students who take standardized tests in the fall could have lost up to 4-6 weeks of learning each school year (when compared with test results from the previous spring). This means that teachers end up dedicating the first month of each new school year for reviewing material before they can move onto any new content and concepts.

The three areas that suffer most from summer learning loss are in the areas of vocabulary/reading, spelling, and math. In Stop! In the Name of Education: Prevent Summer Learning Loss With 7 Simple Steps, we discussed some activities parents could use with children to prevent summer slide. Let's add to that list with even more ways to keep children engaged and learning – all summer long.

Be sure to check out:

•Your Child's School

Talk to child's teacher, and tell him or her that you'd like to work on your child's academics over the summer. Most teachers will have many suggestions for you.

In addition to the classroom teacher as a resource, talk to the front office staff and guidance counselors. Reading lists and summer programs that are organized through the school district may be available for your family, and these staff members can usually point you in the right direction.

•Your Community

A quick Google search for "free activities for kids in (insert your town's name)" will yield results of possible educational experiences and opportunities in your area. Some towns offer "dollar days", park lunches, and local arts and entertainment.

You may even wish to involve your child in the research process to find fun, affordable memberships and discounts to use at area attractions. For New Jerseyans and Coloradans, check out www.funnew-jersey.com and www.colorado.com for ideas.

Of course, don't forget your local library! In addition to books, you can borrow movies and audiobooks, check out the latest issue of your favorite magazine, and get free Internet access on the library's computers. Most libraries offer a plethora of other educational choices, too – from book clubs and author visits to movie nights and crafts classes, you're sure to find something at your local branch that your child will enjoy.

•Stores

This is an extremely engaging activity – and your child won't even know he or she is learning! For grocery shopping, ask your child to write the list while you dictate. At the store, your son/daughter can locate the items and keep a cost tally to stay within a specified budget. At the checkout, you can have a contest to see whose estimate of the final bill is most accurate – and then reward the winner!

You may wish to plan a home improvement project or plant a garden: for this, your child can make the list, research the necessary materials, and then plan and execute the project after a visit to your local home improvement store. All of these activities involve those three critical areas of spelling, vocabulary/reading, and math.

•The Kitchen

This is one of the best places to try new things – by researching new foods, recipes, and discussing healthy food choices – while practicing math skills (such as measuring ingredients, doubling recipes, etc.). Your child may also enjoy reading about new cultures and ethnicities and then trying out some new menu items from those cultures.

•The Television

TV doesn't have to be mind numbing … when used appropriately. You can watch sports with your child to review stats and make predictions; watch documentaries; or tune into the History Channel, Discovery, National Geographic, HGTV, and more. Anything that teaches, helps your child discover new interests, and promotes learning new things together is fair game.

As an extension, you may decide to research whether or not the show portrays accurate information. And for those children who really get "into" a certain topic, you can enrich their learning by taking related trips to the museum, doing Internet research, and checking out books from the library that tie into the topic of interest.

•Movies

Movies can be educational, too, if you debrief with your child afterwards. Schedule a family movie night, and then discuss how realistic the movie was, what the messages were, etc.

For book-based movies (such as Judy Moody, Harry Potter, Percy Jackson, etc.), you could read the book together first, and then view the movie version. Comparing and contrasting the two is another terrific educational way to enjoy time together and work on your child's reasoning skills.

Note: www.imdb.com and www.commonsensemedia.org are great sites for movie recommendations and movie reviews for kids and families.

•Games

Playing games promotes taking turns, reading and math skills, and strategy development. Scour yard sales for affordable board games like Scrabble, Monopoly, Uno, Battleship, and Qwirkle.

Don't forget about non-board games, like those found on the Wii, Nintendo, Xbox, and other gaming consoles. You'll still want to choose wisely and limit your child's screen time, but these electronic versions of popular (and new) games mirror the way kids think ... while focusing on reading and math skills. For more ideas, Google "education apps" for suggestions.

•Books, books, books!

Of course, nothing beats reading for maintaining skills. When you can connect your child with a book that is of interest to him or her, it can be fun for your child, build confidence, and improve fluency.

To help your child find a book that's "just right", use the five-finger rule: choose a page from a possible book and have your child read that page. Every time he or she encounters an unknown word, put up a finger. If your child exceeds five fingers (that is, five unknown words), that book is probably too challenging and he or she may wish to pass on it.

For reluctant readers, consider non-book reading options, like:magazines (such as Ranger Rick, American Girl, Discovery Kids, and Sports Illustrated for Kids), cereal boxes, billboards, current events, closed captioning, and karaoke. If you keep your eyes open, you'll find there are many natural reading opportunities that surround us every day.

Whatever you do, remember to keep it fun. Summer is a time for rest and rejuvenation, and learning doesn't always have to be scheduled. In fact, some of the most educational experiences are unplanned.

Visit lumoslearning.com/parents/summer-program for more information.

Valuable Learning Experiences: A Summer Activity Guide for Parents

Soon school will be out of session, leaving the summer free for adventure and relaxation. However, it's important to also use the summer for learning activities. Giving your son or daughter opportunities to keep learning can result in more maturity, self-growth, curiosity, and intelligence. Read on to learn some ways to make the most of this summer.

Read

Summer is the perfect time to get some extra reading accomplished. Youth can explore books about history, art, animals, and other interests, or they can read classic novels that have influenced people for decades. A lot of libraries have summer fun reading programs which give children, teens, and adults little weekly prizes for reading books. You can also offer a reward, like a $25 gift card, if your child reads a certain amount of books.

Travel

"The World is a book and those who do not travel read only a page." This quote by Saint Augustine illustrates why travel is so important for a student (and even you!). Travel opens our eyes to new cultures, experiences, and challenges. When you travel, you see commonalities and differences between cultures.

Professor Adam Galinsky of Columbia Business School, who has researched travel benefits, said in a Quartz article that travel can help a child develop compassion and empathy: "Engaging with another culture helps kids recognize that their own egocentric way of looking at the world is not the only way of being in the world."

If the student in your life constantly complains about not having the newest iPhone, how would they feel seeing a child in a third-world country with few possessions? If you child is disrespectful and self-centered, what would they learn going to Japan and seeing a culture that promotes respect and otherness instead of self-centeredness?

If you can't afford to travel to another country, start a family travel fund everyone can contribute to and in the meantime, travel somewhere new locally! Many people stay in the area they live instead of exploring. Research attractions in your state and nearby states to plan a short road trip to fun and educational places!

Visit Museums

You can always take your children to visit museums. Spending some quality time at a museum can enhance curiosity because children can learn new things, explore their interests, or see exhibits expanding upon school subjects they recently studied. Many museums have seasonal exhibits, so research special exhibits nearby. For example, "Titanic: The Artifact Exhibition" has been making its way to various museums in the United States. It contains items recovered from the Titanic as well as interactive activities and displays explaining the doomed ship's history and tragic demise. This year, the exhibit is visiting Las Vegas, Orlando, and Waco.

Work

A final learning suggestion for the summer is for students to get a job, internship, or volunteer position. Such jobs can help with exploring career options. For example, if your child is thinking of becoming a vet, they could walk dogs for neighbors, or if your child wants to start their own business, summer is the perfect time to make and sell products.

Not only will a job or volunteer work look good on college applications, but it will also teach your children valuable life lessons that can result in more maturity and responsibility. You could enhance the experience by teaching them accounting and illustrating real world problems to them, like budgeting money for savings and bills.

The above suggestions are just four of the many ways you can help learning continue for your child or children all summer long. Experience and seeing things first-hand are some of the most important ways that students can learn, so we hope you find the above suggestions helpful in designing a fun, educational, and rewarding summer that will have benefits in and out of the classroom.

Additional Information

What if I buy more than one Lumos Study Program?

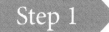 **Step 1**

Visit the URL and login to your account.
http://www.lumoslearning.com

 Step 2

Click on 'My tedBooks' under the "Account" tab.
Place the Book Access Code and submit.

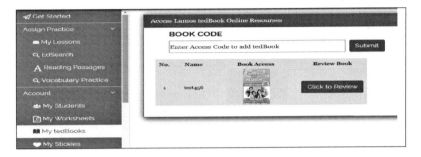

Step 3

To add the new book for a registered student, choose the
⚪ Existing Student button and select the student and submit.

> **Access Lumos tedBook Online Resourses**
>
> **BOOK CODE**
>
> SLHG9-10ML-18526-P
>
> **Assign To** ⓘ
>
> ⚪ Existing Student   ⚪ Add New student

To add the new book for a new student, choose the ⚪ Add New student
button and complete the student registration.

> **Access Lumos tedBook Online Resourses**
>
> **Assign To** ⓘ
>
> ⚪ Existing Student   🔘 Add New student
>
> **Student Name:***   Enter First Name   Enter Last Name
>
> **Student Login***
>
> **Password***
>
> **Submit**

Lumos tedBooks for State Assessments Practice

Lumos tedBook for standardized test practice provides necessary grade-specific state assessment practice and skills mastery. Each tedBook includes hundreds of standards-aligned practice questions and online summative assessments that mirror actual state tests.

The workbook provides students access to thousands of valuable learning resources such as worksheets, videos, apps, books, and much more.

Lumos Learning tedBooks for State Assessment	
SBAC Math & ELA Practice Book	CA, CT, DE, HI, ID, ME, MI, MN, NV, ND, OR, WA, WI
NJSLA Math & ELA Practice Book	NJ
ACT Aspire Math & ELA Practice Book	AL, AR
IAR Math & ELA Practice Book	IL
FSA Math & ELA Practice Book	FL
PARCC Math & ELA Practice Book	DC, NM
GMAS Math & ELA Practice Book	GA
NYST Math & ELA Practice Book	NY
ILEARN Math & ELA Practice Book	IN
LEAP Math & ELA Practice Book	LA
MAP Math & ELA Practice Book	MO
MAAP Math & ELA Practice Book	MS
AZM2 Math & ELA Practice Book	AZ
MCAP Math & ELA Practice Book	MD
OST Math & ELA Practice Book	OH
MCAS Math & ELA Practice Book	MA
CMAS Math & ELA Practice Book	CO
TN Ready Math & ELA Practice Book	TN
STAAR Math & ELA Practice Book	TX
NMMSSA Math & ELA Practice Book	NM

Available

- At Leading book stores
- www.lumoslearning.com/a/lumostedbooks

Made in the USA
Middletown, DE
01 June 2022

66473149R00135